Stuff You Learned At School But Were Afraid You'd Forgotten

EBURY
PRESS

GRAMMAR

The apostrophe

English is unusual in that it allows us two ways of indicating possession. We can do it the French way, e.g. *The tail of the dog*, or we can use an apostrophe, e.g. *The dog's tail*. Similarly, we can use an apostrophe to indicate a missing letter when abbreviating two words, e.g. *don't* instead of *do not*. Many people, however, misguidedly use an apostrophe to indicate the plural, just because it looks correct. Do you know your possessive from your plural?

Rewrite the following using an apostrophe where necessary:

1. The pen of my father _____
2. One week of holidays _____
3. Stamps are sold by the Smiths _____
4. It is cold outside _____
5. Muddy paws on four dogs _____
6. I like the books of Charles Dickens _____
7. Who is the owner of these apples? _____
8. The babies belonging to the women _____
9. The contents found in it _____
10. More than one disco held here _____
11. The cats belonging to Mrs Smith _____
12. It is important to look at the features of it _____
13. More than one page in the books _____
14. Do not miss the races every Saturday _____

LITERATURE

Match these characters to the novel in which they appeared:

Ebenezer Scrooge	1.	• A *Animal Farm*
Bigwig	2.	• B The *His Dark Materials* trilogy
Severus Snape	3.	• C *A Room with a View*
Count Vronsky	4.	• D *Watership Down*
Lyra Belacqua	5.	• E *The Hitchhiker's Guide to the Galaxy*
Napoleon	6.	• F *Lolita*
Dolores Haze	7.	• G *A Christmas Carol*
Ford Prefect	8.	• H *Anna Karenina*
Atticus Finch	9.	• I The *Harry Potter* books
Lucy Honeychurch	10.	• J *To Kill a Mockingbird*

MATHS

Sarah, who's a big fan of Leonardo DiCaprio, has been given a new widescreen plasma TV by David. It has a 16:9 format, which means that the ratio between the picture height and its width is 16:9.

1. If the height of the screen is 62.2cm, what is its width?

_____

2. What is the length of its diagonal?

_____

3. Sarah is watching *Titanic* on her new TV for the 42nd time (the record is held by a Japanese girl, who has seen the film 134 times). The format of the DVD is 2.35 (i.e. 2.35:1). This means that the width of the picture is the same as that of the TV screen.

a. What is the height of the picture?

_____

b. Sarah can see a horizontal black band above and below the TV picture.

What is the height of each of these bands?

_____

c. What percentage of the TV screen's surface is used up by the picture?

_____

There are 20 bags of gold and a set of scales in a room.
One of these 20 bags contains fake coins. The bags don't necessarily have the same number of coins in them (but each one contains at least 30). The real coins weigh 5 grams each and the fake ones 4 grams each. With a single weighing, you need to discover which bag contains the fake coins. How on earth are you going to do it?

* You'll find some useful mathematical formulas to help you solve these problems in the detachable centre section of this book.

HISTORY

Study this famous conclusion to a wartime speech and answer the following questions:

1 Who made this speech?
a. Neville Chamberlain
b. General Montgomery
c. Winston Churchill

2 When was this speech made?
a. June1940
b. July 1941
c. August 1942

3 Who was the ruler of England at this time?
a. George V
b. George VI
c. Edward VIII

4 Who were the Gestapo?
a. German Secret Police
b. German Army
c. German Political Leaders

> Even though large tracts of Europe and many old and famous States have fallen or may fall into the grip of the Gestapo and all the odious apparatus of Nazi rule, we shall not flag or fail.
>
> We shall go on to the end, we shall fight in France,
>
> we shall fight on the seas and oceans,
>
> we shall fight with growing confidence and growing strength in the air, we shall defend our Island, whatever the cost may be,
>
> we shall fight on the beaches,
>
> we shall fight on the landing grounds,
>
> we shall fight in the fields and in the streets,
>
> we shall fight in the hills;
>
> we shall never surrender, and even if, which I do not for a moment believe, this Island or a large part of it were subjugated and starving, then our Empire beyond the seas, armed and guarded by the British Fleet, would carry on the struggle, until, in God's good time, the New World, with all its power and might, steps forth to the rescue and the liberation of the old.

5 What was abbreviated as *Nazi* in the UK?
a. National Socialist German Workers party
b. National Zionist German Peoples' party
c. National Society of German Socialist Peoples

6 In this famous speech, which of these words is used least times?
a. We
b. Shall
c. Fight

7 In which month and year did this war finally end?
a. November 1945
b. October 1945
c. September 1945

8 In another famous speech by this man, what did he offer to the British people?
a. Blood, Toil, Sweat and Tears
b. Blood, Endeavour, Sweat and Toil
c. Toil, Sweat, Energy and Blood

GENERAL CULTURE

Find the titles of these films from the quotes and details of their posters (bonus points to those who can name their release dates, within two years):

There are two kinds of people in the world, my friend. Those who have a rope round their neck and those who have the job of doing the cutting.

A boy's best friend is his mother.

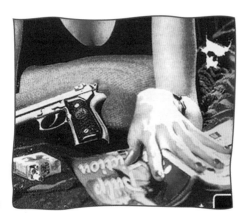

Hamburgers. The cornerstone of any nutritious breakfast.

&GRAMMAR

Figures of speech

We use them without even realizing it. For example:

Metaphor implicitly changes the meaning of a word with another meaning: *All the world's a stage...*

Metonymy substitutes a word referring to an attribute for the thing that is meant: *the crown*, used to refer to a monarch.

Antonomasia replaces a proper noun with a title or epithet, and vice versa: *My hairdresser is a real Romeo!*

Euphemism replaces an offensive word or phrase with one that is judged to be less crude or hurtful: *She passed away.*

Hyperbole is deliberate exaggeration of an idea used for effect: *Let's get to the canteen, I'm dying of hunger...*

Litotes is understating something to mean more: *That Alice Baker, she's not ugly...*

1 Can you recognize the figures of speech used in the following sentences:

My old school friend has already told me that story a thousand times. _____

The suits are out for lunch again! _____

JH, dark and handsome but vertically challenged, seeks attractive female... _____

If she's not home by midnight, she'll be toast! _____

Bill Gates isn't short of a bob or two! _____

He fancies himself as a real John Travolta. _____

2 Describe the person nearest to you at the moment using these figures of speech, which you now have 'at the tip of your tongue'...

LITERATURE

Librarians are often asked for strange book titles. Here are some classic mistakes made by (fictitious) readers. Can you find the correct titles?

1 _____
2 _____
3 _____
4 _____
5 _____
6 _____
7 _____
8 _____
9 _____
10 _____
11 _____
12 _____
13 _____
14 _____

MATHS

Look at this triangle carefully. It's a very straightforward one. Draw the perpendicular segment that goes from each vertex of the triangle to the line containing the opposite side to that vertex. Well done! You've just drawn the three altitudes of the triangle.

1 Let A' be the intersection between the height from A to the side BC, B' the point of intersection between the height from B to the side AC, and C' the point of intersection between the height from C and the side AB.
Compare the products: AA' x BC, BB' x AC et CC' x AB.

2 Let △ be the parallel line to BC through A, and M a point somewhere on this line (but distinct from A).
Now let's look at the triangle MBC.
Draw the altitude of this triangle passing via M.
Let M' be the point of intersection between BC and this height.
Compare AA' and MM' as well as the areas ABC and MBC.

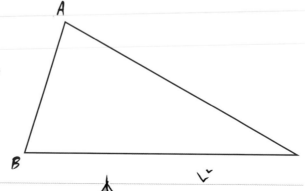

4

FRENCH

2 Fill in the amount in words on this monthly pay cheque for footballer David Beckham.

Numbers

Vingt and **cent** take an **-s** when they're not followed by another number (*deux cents*), otherwise they're invariable (*deux cent trois, quatre-vingt-dix*). **Mille** is always invariable, unlike **million** and **milliard**. A hyphen is used only between numbers under **cent** when they're not already joined by the conjunction **et** (*soixante-huit étudiants, vingt et un policiers*).

3 028 874, 20 €

à _David Beckham_

À _____ le _____

signature :

1 Write out in full the speed of these animals:

Cheval (horse), 70 km/h : *Soixante-dix km/h*

Antilope (antelope), 98 km/h : _____

Guépard (cheetah), 121 km/h: _____

Kangourou (kangaroo), 72 km/h: _____

Chat (cat), 43 km/h: _____

GENERAL CULTURE

The mascots from previous Olympic Games are often forgotten. See if you can find the city and the year of each Games from the following clues.

Nadia Comaneci obtains 10.0 on the assymetric bars. The host country does not win a single gold medal. Frenchman Guy Drut wins in the 110m hurdles. In football, Germany defeats Poland.

Amik

Year _____ / City _____

Mohammed Ali lights the Olympic torch. Jean Galfione gets the gold medal in pole vaulting with a jump of 5.92m. American Michael Johnson and Frenchman Marie-José Perec both win in the 200m/400m double.

Izzy

Year _____ / City _____

Carl Lewis wins in the 100m, the 200m, the long jump and the 4 x 100m relay. Chinese athlete Xu Haifenga obtains the first ever gold medal for his country in the pistol (60 shots) event. The USSR boycott the games following the American boycott of the Moscow Olympics.

Sam

Year _____ / City _____

Steffi Graf wins the Olympic title in tennis and the Grand Slam in the same year. Frenchman Marc Alexandre becomes judo champion in the lightweight (-71kg) category. Sprinter Ben Johnson is disqualifed for drug violations, losing his 100m title to Carl Lewis.

Hodori

Year _____ / City _____

Badminton and female judo become Olympic disciplines for the first time. Marie-José Perec runs the 400m in 48"83. The male basketball event is opened to professional players.

Cobi

Olly, Syd and Millie

Cathy Freeman lights the Olympic torch and takes the gold in the 400m. Swimmer Ian Thorpe wins the 400m freestyle in 3'40" at only 17 years old. In basketball, the French lose against the USA, who keep the title.

Year _____ / City _____

Year _____ / City _____

photos © C.I.O. / Collections du Musée Olympique

LITERATURE

In latin, *incipit* (pronounced *'inkipit'*) means 'it begins', and by extension, that's what we call the first few words of a poem, a song or a book. Match the right book with each incipit:

Renowned curator Jacques Saunière staggered through the vaulted archway of the museum's Grand Gallery **1** •

One of those no-neck monsters hit me with a hot buttered biscuit so I have t'change! **2** •

If you want to find Cherry Tree Lane all you have to do is ask a policeman at the crossroads **3** •

The great fish moved silently through the night water **4** •

Amerigo Bonasera sat in New York Criminal Court Number 3 and waited for justice **5** •

I am always drawn back to the places where I have lived **6** •

Roving has always been, and still is, my ruling passion **7** •

There was no possibility of taking a walk that day **8** •

Happy families are all alike; every unhappy family is unhappy in its own way **9** •

The studio was filled with the rich odour of roses **10** •

When a day that you happen to know is Wednesday starts off by sounding like Sunday, there is something seriously wrong somewhere **11** •

For many days we had been tempest-tossed **12** •

The first place that I can well remember was a large pleasant meadow with a pond of clear water in it **13** •

Nellie, a cruising yawl, swung to her anchor without a flutter of sails, and was at rest **14** •

Call Me Ishmael **15** •

• **A** Oscar Wilde, *The Picture of Dorian Gray*

• **B** P.L. Travers, *Mary Poppins*

• **C** Johann Wyss, *Swiss Family Robinson*

• **D** Leo Tolstoy, *Anna Karenina*

• **E** Truman Capote, *Breakfast at Tiffany's*

• **F** Dan Brown, *The Da Vinci Code*

• **G** Joseph Conrad, *Heart of Darkness*

• **H** Herman Melville, *Moby Dick*

• **I** Peter Benchley, *Jaws*

• **J** Anna Sewell, *Black Beauty*

• **K** Mario Puzo, *The Godfather*

• **L** R.M. Ballantyne, *Coral Island*

• **M** John Wyndham, *Day of the Triffids*

• **N** Tennessee Williams, *Cat on a Hot Tin Roof*

• **O** Charlotte Brontë, *Jane Eyre*

MATHS

Every week, Sarah spends 2 hours, 17 minutes and 24 seconds ironing, 48 minutes and 17 seconds vacuuming, and 84 minutes and 48 seconds washing up. And all without making a fuss. Respect!

1 How much time does she spend on housework every week?

2 How much time does this represent over one year?

3 How many viewings of *Titanic* does that represent? (Film running time: 194 minutes.)

4 How much time would it take her if her husband helped her?

Brunnhilda has 2 wicks, a lighter, and a rather unusual name.
Each wick takes an hour to burn, but doesn't burn consistently. In other words, if half a wick is used up, that doesn't necessarily mean that half an hour has passed. How can you tell when exactly 45 minutes are up using only the wicks and the lighter?

bizzz bizzzz...

GEOGRAPHY

What sort of geographer are you? Here's a quiz that will enable you to find out...

Physical geography

1 What's the name given to the study of landforms?
a. Geomorphology
b. Geodesy
c. Mountainology

2 Which of these rivers forms an estuary when it reaches the sea?
a. The Rhône
b. The Seine
c. The Nile

3 Which climatic phenomenon is characterized by high atmospheric pressure?
a. Cyclone
b. Anticyclone
c. Depression

4 What is the Arabic word for 'desert'?
a. Erg
b. Sahara
c. Lozère

Human geography

1 What crop is grown in Asia on terraces?
a. Wheat
b. Barley
c. Rice

2 What is a town centre called in North America?
a. Central district
b. Central business district
c. Central economic district

3 As what are the attractive southern regions of the USA collectively known?
a. Sun belt
b. Oil belt
c. Ol' south belt

4 Which of the following is not taken into account when measuring the human development of a country?
a. Its wealth
b. Its level of education
c. Its health

Political geography

1 The Security Council of the UN is made up of the victors of...
a. World War I
b. World War II
c. The Hundred Years' War

2 Which of these organizations is situated in South America?
a. NAFTA
b. NATO
c. MERCOSUR

3 The OPEC groups together countries that export...
a. Petroleum
b. Paper
c. Poultry

4 What percentage of the total worldwide expenditure on defence does the USA represent?
a. 10%
b. 20%
c. 50%

SCIENCE

A human skeleton is made up of 206 bones. Here are 20 of them for you to position correctly:

Clavicle, coccyx, vertebral column, ribs, cranium, ulna, femur, humerus, mandible, scapula, ilium, nasal bone, zygomatic bone, fibula, phalanx, radius, patella, sacrum, sternum, tibia.

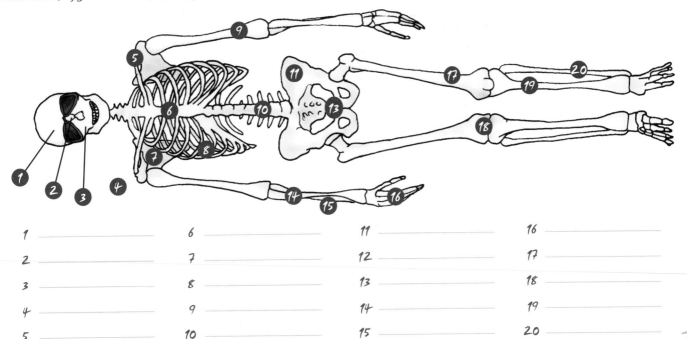

1 _____
2 _____
3 _____
4 _____
5 _____

6 _____
7 _____
8 _____
9 _____
10 _____

11 _____
12 _____
13 _____
14 _____
15 _____

16 _____
17 _____
18 _____
19 _____
20 _____

Know yourself

As those who have read *In Search of Lost Time* will know, Marcel Proust asked himself lots of questions. He even devised a personality test that has become world famous. Now here's your chance to take the test!

The principal aspect of my personality: _____

The quality I most desire in a man: _____

The quality I most desire in a woman : _____

What I like most about my friends : _____

My main fault: _____

My favourite occupation: _____

My dream of happiness: _____

What would be my greatest misfortune: _____

What I should like to be: _____

The country where I would like to live: _____

My favourite colour: _____

My favourite flower: _____

My favourite bird: _____

My favourite prose authors: _____

My favourite poets: _____

My heroes in fiction: _____

My favourite heroines in fiction: _____

My favourite composers: _____

My favourite painters: _____

My heroes in real life: _____

My heroines in history: _____

My favourite names: _____

What I hate most of all: _____

Historical figures that I most despise: _____

The military event that I most admire : _____

The reform that I most admire: _____

The gift of nature that I would like to have: _____

How I would like to die: _____

My present state of mind: _____

Faults for which I have the most indulgence: _____

My motto: _____

what on earth?!

The Eiffel Tower seen from a tank

A 40-pound hamburger

A nudist looking for his contact lenses

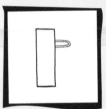

A trombone player in a telephone kiosk

A giant cow

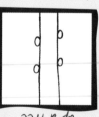

A bear climbing up a tree

A non-ratified tennis ball

Eye strain?

Hermann's grid illusion was discovered more than 100 years ago. If you can't see anything strange about it, get an appointment with your optician quickly, before it's too late...

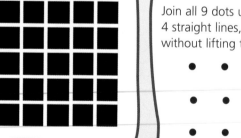

Test 1

Join all 9 dots using only 4 straight lines, and without lifting the pencil.

Oh my God !

Look carefully at the 4 points in the centre for 30 seconds, then try to fix your gaze on a surface around you (a wall, for example). Focus, wait... then share the good news with those around you!

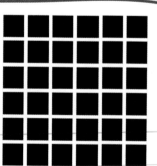

Mission impossible

The aim of this game is to read aloud, as quickly as possible, the colour of the words rather than the words themselves.

Blue Blue Green Blue Blue Blue Red
Red Yellow Blue Green Red Yellow Blue
Green Red Yellow Yellow Yellow Blue Blue
Yellow Red Red Yellow Green Red Green
Red Blue Green Green Red Green Blue
Yellow Yellow Green Green Yellow Red Yellow
Green Red Red Blue Yellow Green Red

Wonky Wall?

Despite appearances, these lines are completely parallel! The diagram is known as the 'cafe wall' because the illusion was first discovered in the pattern of tiles on the outside wall of an English café.

Test 2

Which is the favourite pastime or job of each of these beach-lovers?
surfing, roller-skating, pétanque, shrimp-fishing, lifeguard, selling doughnuts.

1 _____
2 _____
3 _____
4 _____
5 _____
6 _____

Know yourself 2

Bernard Pivot, the 'literary Pope of French television', was inspired by Proust's questionnaire to form his own list of questions, which he posed to guests on his cult TV show. Try to answer them without thinking about them too hard, and compare your answers with those of your friends!

Your favourite word: _____

The word that you hate the most: _____

Your favourite drug: _____

The sound or noise that you most like: _____

The sound or noise that you most hate: _____

Your favourite swear word: _____

The man or woman you think should feature on a new bank note: _____

The job that you would least like to have done: _____

The plant, tree or animal you would like to be reincarnated as: _____

If God exists, what would you like to hear him say to you after you die? _____

SCIENCE

Chemistry

1 What is the chemical process whereby a solid forms a vapour without appearing in the liquid form?
a. Claymation
b. Sublimation
c. Collimation

2 Which zinc compound is the active ingredient of the skin-soothing liquid known as calamine lotion?
a. Zinc Oxide
b. Zinc Carbonate
c. Zinc Sulphate

3 Particles consisting of two or more atoms bonded together are known by what name?
a. Diatoms
b. Ions
c. Molecules

4 Which element takes its name from the Greek word for lead?
a. Molybdenum
b. Lithium
c. Platinum

Physics

1 What is the force that produces rotation?
a. Centripetal
b. Torque
c. Centrifugal

2 Which is the only one of the seven base S.I. units to be defined in terms of a physical artefact?
a. Metre
b. Kilogram
c. Second

3 What is the term used to describe the minimum mass of fissile material that will sustain a nuclear chain reaction?
a. Critical Mass
b. Chain Mass
c. Optimum Decay Mass

4 After whom is a generator devised to produce an electrostatic charge by using a vertical endless belt and large dome named?
a. Van De Hoek
b. Van Der Moolen
c. Van De Graaff

Biology

1 In medicine, a sphygmomanometer measures what?
a. Eyesight
b. Liver Function
c. Blood Pressure

2 Anaerobic exercise produces which acid in muscles?
a. Lactic
b. Peptic
c. Ascorbic

3 The duodenum, jejunum and ileum comprise which organ found in the human body?
a. Pancreas
b. Small Intestine
c. Liver

4 The human heart has four chambers: two auricles and two what?
a. Ventricles
b. Pericardia
c. Mitrals

MATHS

Mark's latest CD is about to be released. He's contracted to receive royalties of 12% of the £15 fixed retail price. After discussion with the marketing deparment of his record company, he's decided to donate 24p from each CD sold to charity, which should increase the overall sales by 25% if the media talk about it.

1 How much would Mark have earned for each CD?

2 How much will he now earn for each CD?

3 Mark originally expected to sell 83,000 copies of the CD. How much will his big heart bring him in now?

4 What is the minimum number of CDs he will have to sell in order not to lose money and so that his generosity costs him nothing?

5 Finally, Mark's decided to give up. Why?

There are three switches on a wall, but the three lights that they operate are in a room on the floor above (following this error, an architect found himself on the dole). How can you find which switch operates each light without having to go upstairs more than once?

HISTORY

History is punctuated with famous sayings. Can you match the quotation with the person?

Oscar Wilde

a. *I am the state.*

Louis XIV

b. *Better to remain silent and be thought a fool than to speak out and remove all doubt.*

Abraham Lincoln

c. *The die has been cast.*

Joan of Arc

d. *An appeaser is one who feeds a crocodile, hoping it will eat him last.*

Julius Caesar

e. *Impossible is a word to be found only in the dictionary of fools.*

Queen Victoria

f. *I am not afraid...I was born to do this.*

Napoleon

g. *I am not young enough to know everything.*

Winston Churchill

h. *Great events make me quiet and calm; it is only trifles that irritate my nerves.*

GENERAL CULTURE

Someone once decribed tennis as boxing with rackets. He wasn't exaggerating...

1 Steffi Graf won the Grand Slam in:

a. 1986 b. 1988 c. 1990

2 What's the name of the venue for the Australian Open?

a. Kooyong b. Melbourne Park c. Meriadeck

3 The Four Musketeers were Borotra, Cochet, Lacoste and...

a. Pêche b. Brugnon c. Abricot

4 What's the other name for the US Open?

a. Flushing Meadows b. Indian Wells c. Key Biscayne

5 What nationality is Gabriela Sabatini?

a. Spanish b. Argentinian c. American

6 Which of these players isn't left-handed?

a. Thomas Muster b. John McEnroe c. Jim Courier

7 Which player holds the record for the fastest serve (155mph)?

a. Goran Ivanisevic b. Andy Roddick c. Mark Philippoussis

8 How many times has Navratilova won Wimbledon?

a. 7 b. 8 c. 9

9 Yannick Noah won the French Open against...

a. Ivan Lendl b. Mats Wilander c. Victor Pecci

10 In 2004, Fabrice Santoro beat Arnaud Clément in...

a. 6h 35min b. 52min c. 3h 33min

11 Who said 'I just play for fun'?

a. Maria Sharapova b. Anastasia Miskina c. Anna Kournikova

12 How old was Michael Chang when he won the French Open?

a. 16 years, 6 months b. 17 years, 3 months c. 18 years, 1 month

13 Who was nicknamed 'The Big Cat'?

a. Miloslav Mecir b. Mickael Pernfors c. Pat Cash

14 Which of these players has a one-handed backhand?

a. Roger Federer b. André Agassi c. Raphaël Nadal

15 Which of these spins?

a. Side spin b. Turbo spin c. Hover spin

16 Henri Leconte is...

a. Right-handed b. Left-handed c. Both

&GRAMMAR

Match up the following sayings with their true sense.

A bird in the hand is worth two in the bush — 1.

A stitch in time saves nine — 2.

Look before you leap — 3.

New brooms sweep clean — 4.

It's like looking for a needle in a haystack — 5.

A loaded wagon makes no noise — 6.

Too many cooks spoil the broth — 7.

Clothes don't make the man — 8.

Don't count your chickens before they are hatched — 9.

He who pays the piper calls the tune — 10.

A • New workers are zealous and often keen to make changes

B • Appearances can be deceptive

C • It's very difficult if not impossible to find something

D • Fix it now and you'll save yourself a lot more work later

E • Work is more efficient with fewer people

F • It's unwise to rely on something that hasn't yet happened

G • Something you have is more valuable than the things you only hope to get

H • The one who foots the bill has the control

I • Consider well before you act; avoid doing anything hasty

J • People with real money don't talk about it

LITERATURE

Which literary works took place in the following fictional places:

1 Brobdingnag, Lilliput and Laputa _____

2 Skull Island _____

3 Mirkwood and The Lonely Mountain _____

4 Llareggub _____

5 Never-Never Land _____

6 Eastasia, Eurasia and Oceania _____

7 Vulgaria _____

8 Syldavia, Borduria, Khemed, San Theordoros _____

9 Ape Kingdom _____

10 Jabberwocky Wood _____

11 The Celestial City and Vanity Fair _____

12 Cyclops' Island and Calypso's Isle _____

13 Maple White Island _____

14 Isla Nubar _____

15 Coketown _____

MATHS

Three young drummers returning from battle have found work in a warehouse, where they unload 4 lorries in 2 hours 40 minutes.

1 How many hours would it take a single drummer to unload 4 lorries? _____

2 How long would it take 1 drummer to unload 1 lorry? _____

3 How many hours would it take 3 drummers to unload 3 lorries? _____

4 How many lorries could 2 drummers unload in 7 hours? _____

5 How could they save time? _____

Three friends take a room in a hotel. Each one pays £10. As they are nice guys, the manger decides to give them a discount of £5. He calls the bellboy and asks him to give the £5 to the guests, but as the young man doesn't know how to divide the £5 into 3, he decides to keep £2 for himself, giving £1 to each of the three men. So, each of these guests has paid £9 for his room. But 9 x 3 = £27, and 27 + 2 = £29. So what on earth has happened to the other pound?

FRENCH

tuvasyarriver.com

Choose the correct translation:

1 C'est la croix et la bannière
a. It's the cross and the banner
b. It's the devil's own work
c. It's too stupid for words

2 He is a queer fish
a. C'est bien fait pour lui
b. Ce poisson n'est pas frais
c. C'est un drôle de type

3 J'ai une ampoule au pied
a. I have a bulb at my foot
b. I have a blistered foot
c. My foot has gone to sleep

4 You have egg on your face
a. C'est bien fait pour vous
b. Vous vous êtes couvert de ridicule
c. Va te faire cuire un œuf

5 Il n'y a pas de quoi fouetter un chat
a. I have a finger in the pie
b. Nothing to whip a cat with
c. Nothing to make a fuss about

6 I get cold feet
a. Je me sens de trop
b. J'ai froid aux pieds
c. J'ai la frousse

7 Avoir un verre dans le nez
a. To be wearing glasses
b. To have had one over the eight
c. To be buttered up

8 Keep you nose clean
a. Tu as le nez qui coule
b. Tiens toi à carreau
c. Pour qui tu te prends

9 Avoir très faim
a. To be starving
b. To have a wolf's hunger
c. To be stoned

10 There is a snake in the grass
a. Il y a une anguille sous roche
b. J'ai des fourmis dans les jambes
c. Il y a un serpent dans l'herbe

11 C'est une oie blanche
a. She is a white goose
b. She is wet behind the ears
c. She has her head in the clouds

12 I am in the stew
a. Je suis dans le ragoût
b. Je suis dans tous mes états
c. Je donne ma langue au chat

13 J'en bave des ronds de chapeau
a. I have my tongue hanging out
b. I ran into a snag
c. I am flabbergasted

14 I am playing gooseberry
a. Je ne suis pas né de la dernière pluie
b. Je me sens de trop
c. Je suis prêt à tout

15 Quand les poules auront des dents
a. They make no bones about it
b. When the devil is blind
c. When the rivers will be dry

GENERAL CULTURE

Find the name of the group and the album from a detail of the album sleeve and the names of 2 of their songs.

A day in the life
With a little help from my friends

Group _____
Album _____

Parachute woman
Sympathy for the devil

Group _____
Album _____

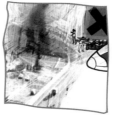

Karma polic
No surprises

Group _____
Album _____

God only knows
Caroline, no

Group _____
Album _____

One
The fly

Group _____
Album _____

Wonderwall
Morning glory

Group _____
Album _____

Stairway to heaven
Black dog

Group _____
Album _____

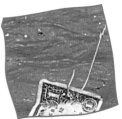

Smells like teen spirit
Come as you are

Group _____
Album _____

13

GEOGRAPHY

Can you position all 50 American states correctly on the map?

Alabama, Alaska, Arizona, Arkansas, California, Colorado, Connecticut, Delaware, Florida, Georgia, Hawaii, Idaho, Illinois, Indiana, Iowa, Kansas, Kentucky, Louisiana, Maine, Maryland, Massachusetts, Michigan, Minnesota, Mississippi, Missouri, Montana, Nebraska, Nevada, New Hampshire, New Jersey, New Mexico, New York, North Carolina, North Dakota, Ohio, Oklahoma, Oregon, Pennsylvania, Rhode Island, South Carolina, South Dakota, Tennessee, Texas, Utah, Vermont, Virginia, Washington, West Virginia, Wisconsin, Wyoming.

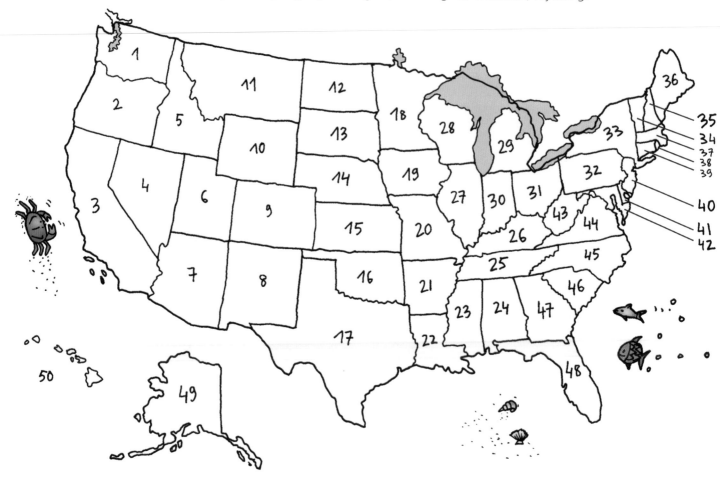

MATHS

Giles has divided his field into 4 plots as shown in the diagram (*fig. 1*), which he has authorized us to reproduce here, following negotiations.

1 What is the total area of alfalfa and the area of wheat in this field, and what can be said about each of the plots of alfalfa?

2 What is the total area of the field? What can be said about $(a + b)^2$?

3 Giles is reorganizing his field (*fig. 2*). Why?

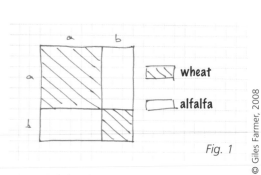

There are 9 gold ingots in a room, one of which is fake and is heavier than the others. How can you find the fake ingot using a pair of scales but with only two weighings?

Fig. 1

Fig. 2

HISTORY

How well connected are you to royalty? Test yourself with these questions on the kings and queens of England:

1 Who demonstrated that he couldn't hold back the tide? _____

2 Who gave up his throne so he could marry a divorcee? _____

3 Who fell at the Battle of Hastings? _____

4 During whose reign did Shakespeare, Bacon and Raleigh prosper? _____

5 Who was the last of the Plantagenets? _____

6 Which King of Mercia had a dyke built from the Wye to the Dee? _____

7 Who was born at Greenwich in 1491? _____

8 Who oversaw the Act of Union between Great Britain and Ireland? _____

9 Who was known as 'The Unready'? _____

10 Which king prompted the murder of Thomas à Becket? _____

11 What was the first name of the king nicknamed 'The Confessor'? _____

12 Who introduced the Magna Carta? _____

13 Whose reign lasted only nine days? _____

14 What was the name of Catherine of Aragon's daughter? _____

15 Who was the victor at the Battle of Tewkesbury? _____

16 Who came to the throne on the death of Cromwell? _____

17 Who ordered the execution of Sir Walter Raleigh? _____

18 Which king ordered the massacre at Glencoe? _____

19 The Gunpowder Plot was hatched to despatch which king? _____

20 Edmund Hillary reached the summit of Everest during whose reign? _____

GENERAL CULTURE

20

These eyes belong to actors in famous TV series. Find their names and the TV series in which they star and, while you're about it, the name of the characters they play:

Aaaaaaah! Something just touched my right leg! Oh no it was only my left leg....

If you want to make jokes then I will pull out your ribcage and wear it as a hat.

It felt pretty personal when you killed my wife.

Tell me what you don't like about yourself.

Bozo the Clown. Do we really need 'the clown'? Are we going to confuse him with Bozo the Pope?

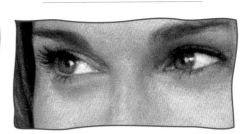

Hi, I'd like a cheeseburger, please, a large fries and a cosmopolitan.

The test of the summer

How perceptive are you about people? And how well do you really know your friends? The aim of this test is to predict how those close to you would react in everyday or unusual situations. Compare your answers with theirs to discover the Freud in your group....

1 **You think back on your schooldays:**
a. With nostalgia
b. With horror
c. Rarely – it's all a blank

2 **At the cinema:**
a. You never cry
b. You cry like a baby
c. You cry, but discreetly

3 **Your family photos are:**
a. In a shoebox
b. Organized in photo albums
c. Scattered all over the place

4 **You prefer:**
a. Milk chocolate
b. Dark chocolate
c. White chocolate

5 **Which comes easiest to you:**
a. Gentleness
b. Firmness
c. Diplomacy

6 **When you are guilty, are you most likely to:**
a. Own up straight away
b. Wait a while
c. Deny it for as long as possible

7 **You think that:**
a. Money can't buy happiness
b. Money = happiness
c. Money can't make you happy but it certainly helps.

8 **In a restaurant, you order your steak:**
a. Well done
b. Medium-rare
c. However it comes

9 **In tennis, the umpire awards you a disputable point:**
a. You refuse it and give the point to your opponent
b. You accept the point
c. You suggest a replay

10 **You are:**
a. Always late
b. Rarely late
c. Never late

11 **If you were in the military, you'd most likely be in:**
a. The army
b. The navy
c. The air force

12 **You have some bad luck. You say:**
a. $#° * •§& * $£@ !!!
b. That's all I needed!
c. Life can be a pain.

13 **When you lie, you do so:**
a. Nervously
b. Wholeheartedly
c. With wild embellishments

14 **What you hate more than anything are:**
a. Funny stories
b. Spoonerism
c. Blonde jokes

15 **Don't leave until tomorrow:**
a. What you can do today
b. What you can leave until the day after
c. What you can get someone else to do

16 **When you're giving blood:**
a. You look at the needle
b. You turn your head away
c. You clench your teeth

21 **You prefer children who are aged:**
a. Between 0 and 5 years old
b. Between 5 and 15 years old
c. Older than 15

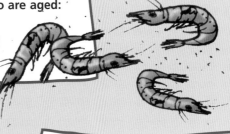

17 **There's a problem with a dish you've ordered in a restaurant:**
a. You send it back politely
b. You eat it without saying anything
c. You make a scene

22 **At yoyo, you are:**
a. Rubbish
b. OK
c. Excellent

24 **You would like to have lived:**
a. In the Middle Ages
b. In the 17th century
c. In the 19th century

18 **Politically, you are positioned:**
a. On the left
b. In the centre
c. On the right

23 **The musical style you most hate is:**
a. Rap
b. Techno
c. Country

25 **You like to see your friends:**
a. At your home
b. At theirs
c. Out somewhere

19 **For breakfast, you absolutely must have:**
a. Tea or coffee
b. Hot chocolate or milk
c. Orange juice

20 **You would love to have been:**
a. Luciano Pavarotti (or María Callas)
b. Al Pacino (or Sharon Stone)
c. David Beckham (or Kelly Holmes)

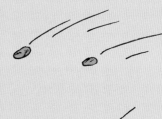

Scores

	1	2	3	4	5	6	7	8	9	10	11	12	13	14	15	16	17	18	19	20	21	22	23	24	25
a.																									
b.																									
c.																									
pts																									

TOTAL 25

&GRAMMAR

Can you and your crew, team or gang of friends match each of these animals with the correct name for a group of them?

Lions **1** •
Owls **2** •
Geese **3** •
Cats **4** •
Dogs **5** •
Hawks **6** •
Horses **7** •
Peacocks **8** •
Pigs **9** •
Rhinoceroses **10** •

Whales **11** •
Toads **12** •
Chickens **13** •
Swans **14** •
Penguins **15** •
Partridges **16** •
Hares **17** •
Foxes **18** •
Crows **19** •
Ants **20** •

• **A** Gaggle
• **B** Herd
• **C** Cast
• **D** Muster
• **E** Cluster
• **F** Parliament
• **G** Kennel
• **H** Drove
• **I** Knot
• **J** School

• **K** Crash
• **L** Pride
• **M** Rookery
• **N** Skulk
• **O** Colony
• **P** Bevy
• **Q** Murder
• **R** Down
• **S** Brood
• **T** Covey

HISTORY

Match up these famous battles with the year in which they took place:

Trafalgar, The Somme, Hastings, Goose Green, Edge Hill, Balaclava, Gettysburg, Stalingrad, Bannockburn, Agincourt.

1314   **1805**   **1863**   **1916**   **1982**

1066   **1415**   **1642**   **1854**   **1942**

MATHS

Mr McDonald owns a retangular field that is 364 metres long and 126 metres wide.

1 What is the area of his field in square metres?

2 To protect his goat, Blanquette, which dreams of escaping, Mr McDonald wants to sink posts all around the perimeter of his field, spacing them at equal distances apart. What will be the minimum space between two posts?

3 How many intervals between posts will there be along one length of the field? And how many along its width?

4 How many posts will there be along each length? And along each width?

5 How many posts will there be in all?

6 Finally, Mr McDonald uses the wood from the posts to fuel his fire? Why?

In the port of Amsterdam is moored a yacht, at the stern of which is a 10m ladder. The rungs of this ladder are spaced 20cm apart. The sea has reached the third rung and is rising by 40cm an hour. Which rung will the water have reached after 2 hours?

SCIENCE

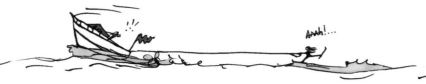

Name these dishes from the descriptions.
To make it easier, we've given you the first letter, A to Z!

A Oysters wrapped in bacon _____

B Scottish dish of oatmeal, soda and salt _____

C Indian flatbread _____

D Vine leaves stuffed with meat and rice _____

E Fried, stuffed pancakes cooked with chilli sauce _____

F Middle-eastern chickpea patties _____

G Stew with okra and rice _____

H Franfurter in a bun _____

I A Turkish dish of stuffed aubergines _____

J Cajun dish of meat, onion, celery and green pepper _____

K Indian ice cream with reduced milk and nuts _____

L Flat pasta dish of minced meat, tomatoes and white cheese _____

M Small sponge cake _____

N French sweet made from almonds and honey _____

O Italian dish of braised knuckle of veal, wine and tomatoes _____

P German, malted rye bread _____

Q French savoury flan with egg, bacon and cheese filling _____

R Indian yoghurt-based cucumber salad _____

S German pickled cabbage _____

T Small appetisers popular in Spain _____

U A hybrid of a grapefruit and a mandarin or tangerine _____

V Potato and leek soup, usually served cold _____

W Crisp, golden-brown pancake with deep indentations _____

X Thickened cream soup garnished with diced chicken _____

Y Bite-sized chicken pieces skewered and grilled, Japanese-style _____

Z Italian dessert made with egg yolks, marsala and sugar _____

GENERAL CULTURE

Find the titles of these films from the quotes and details of their posters
(bonus points to those who can name their release dates, within two years):

At least you'll never be a vegetable, because even an artichoke has a heart.

Toto, I have a feeling we're not in Kansas anymore.

I ate his liver with some fava beans and a nice chianti.

_____   _____   _____

&GRAMMAR

Punctuation

Punctuation (*comma, full stop, inverted commas*, etc.) is often overlooked, even though it carries meaning. In fact, '**the cat, which is miaowing, is thirsty**', does not have the same sense as '**the cat which is miaowing is thirsty**'. So be precise!

1 Modify the meaning of these sentences by adding one or two commas:

The president is not dead as we were told.

My uncle who is a film director is going to move to Cannes.

You will not be paid as agreed.

The French who sing in tune will perform with Celine Dion.

The footballers having travelled by air will be less efficient.

2 Punctuate these sentences.
You'll need to add: 11 , 5 . 3 : 2 ; 4 ' 4 ' 3 ? 2 ! :

Our toaster has two positions ☐ too soon or too late ☐

I don't know how to cook ☐ Use a timer ☐ No ☐ I just rely on the smoke detector ☐

I never ask my wife ☐ ☐ What are you cooking ☐ ☐ ☐

I ask ☐ ☐ What are you defrosting ☐ ☐

I am on a ☐ grapefruit ☐ diet ☐ in other words ☐ I can eat everything except grapefruit ☐

Mushrooms ☐ they're like love ☐ until you've tasted them ☐ you don't know whether or not they're dangerous ☐

My father often said to me ☐ ☐ I'm not vegetarian ☐ but the animals that I eat are ☐ ☐

To put together this table ☐ you will need ☐ a hammer ☐ nails ☐ wood glue and lots of patience ☐

LITERATURE

Reunite these famous literary couples:

Jeanette •	• *War and Peace*	• Aragorn
Jack Twist •	• *Sons and Lovers*	• Andrei Bolkonsky
Catherine Earnshaw •	• *The Lord of the Rings*	• Ennis del Mar
Natasha Rostova •	• *Oranges Are Not the Only Fruit*	• Tom
Tatiana Romanova •	• *Wuthering Heights*	• Charles Smithson
Arwen •	• *The Water Babies*	• Fitzwilliam Darcy
Elizabeth Bennet •	• *The French Lieutenant's Woman*	• James Bond
Ellie •	• *Pride and Prejudice*	• Paul Morel
Clara Dawes •	• *Brokeback Mountain*	• Melanie
Ernestina Freeman •	• *From Russia with Love*	• Heathcliff

MATHS

A little reminder: a whole number is called a prime number if it is greater than 1 and divisible only by 1 and by itself.

1 Find the first 12 prime numbers.

2 Write 280 as a product of prime numbers. Establish the values of a, b and c such that $280 = 2^a \times 5^b \times 7^c$. You will have thus reduced 280 into prime factors – but with half the work having been done for you!

3 Reduce 5425 into prime factors.

Wolfgang and Romulus are two cyclists of more or less equal talent. To decide who is the better cyclist, they decide to hire a tandem. From mile 1 to mile 12, Wolfgang pedals and Romulus, sitting behind, times him. They then change places and roles from mile 12 to mile 24. One of the two friends wins this challenge easily. But who, and more to the point, why?

Maths Memo

for the forgetful generation...

Pythagoras' theorem

In a right-angled triangle, the area of the square whose side is the hypotenuse (the side opposite the right angle, which is also the longest of the three sides) is equal to the sum of the areas of the squares of the other two sides.

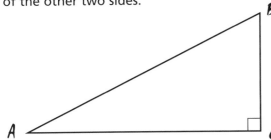

In a triangle ABC where C is a right angle, then $AC^2 + BC^2 = AB^2$

Square root

The square root of number X equals A if A x A = X. It is written $A = \sqrt{X}$

Prime number

A whole number larger than 1 that is divisible only by 1 and by itself. Ex: *2, 3, 5, 7, 11,* etc.

Decomposition into prime factors

To reduce a whole number into prime factors, write this number in the form of a product of prime numbers. E.g. *35 = 5 x 7 or 75 = 3 x 5².*

Circles / Disks

A **circle** is a curved line in which all points are at an equal distance from a point named the **centre**.
A **disk** is the surface defined by a circle.
The **radius** (R) of a circle is the straight line from its centre to its circumference.
The **diameter** (D) joins two points of the circumference of a circle, passing through its centre.
D = 2R, the **perimeter** of a circle = 2πR, the **surface** of a disk = πR² (π = 3.14116).

Area (or surface) of a triangle

To find the area of a triangle, multiply the length of an altitude of the triangle by the length of the opposite side, then divide by 2.

Speed

Speed is the relationship between a **distance (*d*)** and the **time (*t*)** it takes to travel it.
If you know two of the three elements (***s, d, t***), it is easy to work ou the third one.

$$V = \frac{d}{t}$$

Time / Duration

1 day = 24 hours = 1,440 minutes = 86,400 seconds
1 hour = 60 minutes = 3,600 seconds
1 minute = 60 seconds

continued on page VIII

I

Answers

Part 1

p. 2

English Language

My father's pen. One week's holidays. The Smiths sell stamps. It's cold outside. Four dogs' muddy paws. I like Charles Dickens' books. Who's the owner of these apples? The women's babies. Its contents. Discos held here. Mrs Smith's cats. It's important to look at its features. Pages in the books. Don't miss the Saturday races.

Literature

1g, 2d, 3i, 4h, 5b, 6a, 7f, 8e, 9j, 10c.

Maths

1. 62.2 x 16/9 = 110.6 cm.

2. According to the Pythagorean theorem, D = 126.9 cm.

3a. 110.6 / 2.35 = 47.1 cm.

3b. (62.2 – 47.1) / 2 = 7.6 cm.

3c. Usable surface = 62.2 x 110.6 = 6879.3 cm², Surface used = 110.6 x 47.1 = 5209.3 cm², Percentage of the surface used = 5209.3 / 6879.3 = 0.757 = 75.7 %.

4. Take 1 coin from the first bag, 2 coins from the second and so on until the twentieth. You will have 210 coins in all (1 + 2 + 3 +... + 20). In theory, the total weight should be 210 x 5 = 1050 g. Weigh these coins and the difference between the theoretical weight and the actual weight will give you the number of the bag conatining the fake coins. If, for example, they weigh 990 g, you can deduce that the bag containing the fake coins is the fifteenth one (1050 – 990 = 60 g, and 60/4 = 15).

p. 3

History

1c, 2a, 3b, 4a, 5a, 6c, 7c, 8a.

General Culture

The Good, the Bad and the Ugly (1968), *Psycho* (1960), *Pulp Fiction* (1994).

p. 4

English Language

1. Hyperbole, metonymy, euphemism, metaphor, litotes, antonomasia.

Literature

1. *The Old Man and the Sea* **2.** *The Trial* **3.** *As I Lay Dying* **4.** *Barchester Towers* **5.** *Tales of the Unexpected* **6.** *Villette* **7.** *L'Ecole des Femmes* **8.** *The Alchemist* **9.** *Nothing Like the Sun* **10.** *The Potting Shed* **11.** *Mansfield Park* **12.** *The Story of Miss Moppet* **13.** *His Last Bow* **14.** *The Cricket on the Hearth*.

Maths

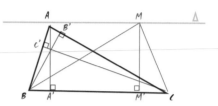

1. The 3 products are all equal to double the volume of the triangle ABC.

2. AA' and MM' are perpendicular to BC, so parallel to each other, which can be written AA' // MM'. Also, AM // A'M', therefore AA'M'M is a parallelogram, which means that AA' = M'M. The surface of ABC = 1/2 x BC x AA', that of MBC = 1/2 x BC x MM', therefore, from what has already been shown, the 2 areas are equal.

p. 5

French

1. Quatre-vingt-dix-huit, cent vingt et un, soixante-douze, quarante-trois.

2. Trois millions vingt-huit mille huit cent soixante-quatorze euros et vingt centimes.

General Culture

AMIK: 1976, Montreal. *IZZY:* 1996, Atlanta.

SAM: 1984, Los Angeles. *HODORI:* 1988, Seoul.

COBI: 1992, Barcelona. *OLLY, SYD AND MILLIE:* 2000, Sydney.

p. 6

Literature

1f, 2n, 3b, 4i, 5k, 6e, 7l, 8o, 9d, 10a, 11m, 12c, 13j, 14g, 15h.

Maths

1. 2 hours, 17 minutes and 24 seconds + 48 minutes, 17 seconds + 84 minutes, 48 seconds = 2 hours, 149 minutes and 89 seconds = 4 hours, 30 minutes and 29 seconds.

2. 4 hours, 30 minutes and 29 seconds x 52 = 8 days, 19 hours, 1 minute and 8 seconds.

3. (8 x 24 x 60) + (19 x 60) + 1 minute + 8 seconds = 12,660 minutes, 8 seconds; 12,660 / 194 = 65.20. Sarah could therefore watch her favourite film 65 times.

4. Not much more.

5. Light one wick at both ends and the second at one end only. After 30 minutes, the first will be burnt up and the other one will have 30 minutes still left to burn. Simply light the other end of this wick, which will be completely burnt up in 15 minutes, 45 minutes from the start of this particularly enlightening experience.

Geography

Physical geography: 1a, 2b, 3b, 4b.
Human geography: 1c, 2b, 3a, 4a.
Political geography: 1b, 2c, 3a, 4c.

Science

1. cranium, **2.** nasal bone,
3. zygomatic bone, **4.** mandible,
5. clavicle, **6.** sternum, **7.** scapula,
8. ribs, **9.** humerus, **10.** vertebral
column, **11.** ilium, **12.** sacrum,
13. coccyx, **14.** radius, **15.** ulna, **16.** phalanx,
17. femur, **18.** patella, **19.** tibia, **20.** fibula.

Test 1

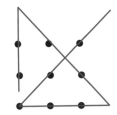

Test 2

1. shrimp-fishing **2.** roller-skating **3.** pétanque **4.** surfing,
5. lifeguard, **6.** selling doughnuts.

Part 2

Science

Chemistry: 1b, 2a, 3c, 4a.
Physics: 1b, 2b, 3a, 4c.
Biology: 1c, 2a, 3b, 4a.

Maths

1. 15 x 0.12 = £1.80.
2. 1.8 – 0.24 = £1.56.
3. Mark should have earned £149,400 (83,000 x 1.8). The number of CDs sold should now be 83,000 x 1.25 = 103,750. Mark will therefore earn 103,750 x 1.56 = £161,850.
4. Let N be the number of CDs Mark would need to sell. He will earn £1.56 for each one. N will therefore need to be at least £149,400, the amount he was originally hoping to earn. Therefore, N = £149,400/1.56 = 95,769.23. Mark will need to sell a minimum of 95,770 CDs.
5. His producer told him he would have to join with punk band the Scuzzbags in order to ensure enough publicity.
6. Let's call the three switches A, B and C. Turn on switch A, then wait for a few minutes (long enough for the bulb to heat up) before switching it off. Switch on B, then go upstairs to see which bulb is lit. The light that is on is therefore linked to switch B, the bulb that is off, but warm, to A, and the bulb that is still cold is operated by switch C. It's really quite simple!

History

1g, 2a, 3b, 4f, 5c, 6h, 7e, 8d.

General Culture

1b, 2b, 3b, 4a, 5b, 6c, 7b, 8c, 9b, 10a, 11c, 12b, 13a, 14a, 15a, 16b (or c).

Grammar

1g, 2d, 3i, 4a, 5c, 6j, 7e, 8b, 9f, 10h

Literature

1. *Gulliver's Travels*, **2.** *King Kong*, **3.** *The Hobbit*, **4.** *Under Milk Wood*, **5.** *Peter Pan*, **6.** *Nineteen Eighty-Four*, **7.** *Chitty Chitty Bang Bang*, **8.** *The Adventures of Tintin*, **9.** *Tarzan of the Apes*, **10.** *Through the Looking Glass*, **11.** *The Pilgrim's Progress*, **12.** *The Odyssey*, **13.** *The Lost World*, **14.** *Jurassic Park*, **15.** *Hard Times*.

Maths

1. 3 x 2h 40 = 8h.
2. 8h / 4 = 2h.
3. The same time it takes 1 drummer to unload 1 lorry, that is 2 hours.
4. In 1 hour, 2 drummers can unload 1 lorry, so in 7 hours, 7 lorries.
5. By unloading their drums!
6. The calculation was incorrect... The price of the room is £30. The discount is £5. The actual cost is therefore 30 – 5 = £25. If you add the £1 given back to each of the guests, and the £2 kept by the bellboy, you have £30.

French

1b, 2c, 3b, 4b, 5c, 6c, 7b, 8b, 9a, 10a, 11b, 12b, 13b, 14b, 15b.

General Culture

The Beatles (*Sgt. Pepper's Lonely Hearts Club Band*), The Rolling Stones (*Beggars Banquet*), Radiohead (*OK Computer*), The Beach Boys (*Pet Sounds*), U2 (*Achtung Baby*), Oasis (*What's the Story, Morning Glory?*), Led Zeppelin (*IV*), Nirvana (*Nevermind*).

p. 14

Geography

1. Washington, 2. Oregon, 3. California, 4. Nevada, 5. Idaho, 6. Utah, 7. Arizona, 8. New Mexico, 9. Colorado, 10. Wyoming, 11. Montana, 12. North Dakota, 13. South Dakota, 14. Nebraska, 15. Kansas, 16. Oklahoma, 17. Texas, 18. Minnesota, 19. Iowa, 20. Missouri, 21. Arkansas, 22. Louisiana, 23. Mississippi, 24. Alabama, 25. Tennessee, 26. Kentucky, 27. Illinois, 28. Wisconsin, 29. Michigan, 30. Indiana, 31. Ohio, 32. Pennsylvania, 33. New York, 34. Vermont, 35. New Hampshire, 36. Maine, 37. Massachusetts, 38. Rhode Island, 39. Connecticut, 40. New Jersey, 41. Delaware, 42. Maryland, 43. West Virginia, 44. Virginia, 45. North Carolina, 46. South Carolina, 47. Georgia, 48. Florida, 49. Alaska, 50. Hawaii.

Maths

1. Alfalfa = 2 ab; wheat = $a^2 + b^2$; the plots are both equal to ab.

2. The area of the field = $a^2 + b^2 + 2ab$; the field being a square of which each side equals a + b, its area is thus $(a+b)^2$. It has thus been shown that $(a + b)^2 = a^2 + b^2 + 2ab$. The same result could have been arrived at by writing $(a + b)^2 = (a + b) \times (a + b)$.

3. So that he can make ham sandwiches.

4. First weighing: 3 ingots on one side of the scales and 3 on the other, leaving 3 to one side. Then, depending on the result, 1, 1 and 1.

p. 15

History

1. Canute, 2. Edward VIII, 3. Harold II, 4. Elizabeth I, 5. Richard III, 6. Offa, 7. Henry VIII, 8. George III, 9. Ethelred II, 10. Henry II, 11. Edward, 12. John, 13. Lady Jane Grey, 14. Mary, 15. Edward IV, 16. Charles II, 17. James I, 18. William III, 19. James I, 20. Elizabeth II.

General Culture

Lisa Kudrow, *Friends*, Phoebe Buffay; **Sarah Michelle Gellar**, *Buffy the Vampire Slayer*, Buffy Summers; **Kiefer Sutherland**, *24*, Jack Bauer; **Julian McMahon**, *Nip/Tuck*, Christian Troy; **Jerry Seinfeld**, *Seinfeld*, Jerry Seinfeld; **Sarah Jessica Parker**, *Sex and the City*, Carrie Bradshaw.

Part 3

p. 18

Grammar

1l, 2f, 3a, 4e, 5g, 6c, 7b, 8d, 9h, 10k, 11j, 12i, 13s, 14p, 15m, 16t, 17r, 18n, 19q, 20o.

History

1066 – Hastings, 1314 – Bannockburn, 1415 – Agincourt, 1642 – Edge Hill, 1805 – Trafalgar, 1854 – Balaclava, 1863 – Gettysburg, 1916 – The Somme, 1942 – Stalingrad, 1982 – Goose Green.

Maths

1. 364 x 126 = 45,864 m².

2. 364 = 22 x 7 x 13; 126 = 2 x 32 x 7. GCD (364,126) = 2 x 7 = 14. The minium space between 2 posts is therefore 14m.

3. The number of intervals along a length is 364/14 = 26. And along each width: 126/14 = 9.

4. The total number of posts = the number of intervals + 1, thus along 1 length = 26 + 1 = 27 posts; along 1 width 9 + 1 = 10 posts.

5. 2 x (26+9) = 70, not 2 x (27+10), otherwise some of the corner posts would be counted twice.

6. While Mr McDonald was working out these calculations, the wolf ate his goat.

7. Still the third, because the boat rises at the same time as the tide. Unanswerable logic…

p. 19

Science

1. Angels on Horseback, 2. Bannock, 3. Chapati, 4. Dolmades, 5. Enchiladas, 6. Falafel, 7. Gumbo, 8. Hot Dog, 9. Imam Bayildi, 10. Jambalaya, 11. Kulfi, 12. Lasagne, 13. Madeleine, 14. Nougat, 15. Osso Bucco, 16. Pumpernickel, 17. Quiche Lorraine, 18. Raita, 19. Sauerkraut, 20. Tapas, 21. Ugli Fruit, 22. Vichyssoise, 23. Waffle, 24. Xavier, 25. Yakitori, 26. Zabaglione.

General Culture

Amelie (2001), *The Wizard of Oz* (1939), *The Silence of the Lambs* (1991).

p. 20

Grammar

1. The president is not dead, as we were told.
My uncle, who is a film director, is going to move to Cannes.
You will not be paid, as agreed.
The French, who sing in tune, will perform with Celine Dion.
The footballers, having travelled by air, will be less efficient.

2. Our toaster has two positions: too soon or too late.
I don't know how to cook. Use a timer? No, I just rely on the smoke detector!
I never ask my wife, 'What are you cooking?'; I ask, 'What are you defrosting?'
I am on a 'grapefruit' diet; in other words, I can eat everything except grapefruit.
Mushroooms, they're like love: until you've tasted them, you don't know whether or not they're dangerous.
My father often said to me, 'I'm not vegetarian, but the animals that I eat are.'
To put together this table, you will need: a hammer, nails, wood glue and lots of patience!

Literature

Jeanette and Melanie, *Oranges Are Not the Only Fruit*; **Jack Twist and Ennis del Mar**, *Brokeback Mountain*; **Catherine Earnshaw and Heathcliff**, *Wuthering Heights*; **Natasha Rostova and Andrei Bolkonsky**, *War and Peace*; **Tatiana Romanova and James Bond**, *From Russia with Love*; **Arwen**

and **Aragorn**, *The Lord of the Rings*; **Elizabeth Bennet and Fitzwilliam Darcy**, *Pride And Prejudice*; **Ellie and Tom**, *The Water Babies*; **Clara Dawes and Paul Morel**, *Sons aand Lovers*; **Ernestina Freeman and Charles Smithson**, *The French Lieutenant's Woman*.

Maths

1. 2, 3, 5, 7, 11, 13, 17, 19, 23, 29, 31, 37.

2. The smallest prime number that divides 280 is 2 (280 = 2 x 140). The quotient of the division 280/2 is 140. Next find the smallest prime number that divides this quotient, and so on. 280 = 2 x 2 x 2 x 5 x 7 = 2^3 x 5 x 7, thus a = 3, b = c = 1.

3. 5425 = 5^2 x 7 x 31.

4. Wolfgang cycles 1 miles less than Romulus (11 miles and 12 miles respectively) because he starts from mile 1 and not from mile 0. He therefore achieves an overwhelming victory, but in an unfair contest, which is, of course, deplorable.

p. 29
Geography

1. Ullapool, 2. Inverness, 3. Aberdeen, 4. Glasgow, 5. Edinburgh, 6. Newcastle, 7. Carlisle, 8. Leeds, 9. Manchester, 10. Sheffield, 11. Chester, 12. Nottingham, 13. Northampton, 14. Milton Keynes, 15. Birmingham, 16. Aberystwyth, 17. Swansea, 18. Cardiff, 19. Gloucester, 20. Bristol, 21. Penzance, 22. Plymouth, 23. Bournemouth, 24. Portsmouth, 25. Brighton, 26. Ipswich, 27. Norwich, 28. Cork, 29. Dublin, 30. Belfast.

p. 30
Science

1. Bear: Sow, Boar, Cub, Den; **2. Mole**: Female, Male, Pup, Fortress; **3. Pigeon**: Hen, Cock, Squab, Loft; **4. Badger:** Sow, Boar, Kit/Cub, Sett/Earth; **5. Lion**: Lion, Lioness, Cub, Den; **6. Horse**: Mare, Stallion, Foal, Stable; **7. Otter**: Female, Male, Whelp, Holt; **8. Fox**: Vixen, Dog, Kit/Cub/Pup, Earth/Lair; **9. Bee**: Drone, Queen, Larva, Hive/Apiary; **10. Eagle**: Female, Male, Eaglet, Eyrie; **11. Hare**: Doe, Buck, Leveret, Form/Down; **12. Wolf**: Bitch, Dog, Pup/Whelp, Lair; **Beaver**: Female, Male, Pup/Kitten, Lodge; **14. Mouse**: Doe, Buck, Pup/Pinkie/Kitten, Hole/Nest; **15. Tiger**: Tigress, Tiger, Cub/Whelp, Lair; **16. Donkey**: Jenny, Jack, Colt/Foal, Stable; **17. Squirrel**: Doe, Buck, Pup/Kit/Kitten, Dray; **18. Dog**: Bitch, Dog, Pup, Kennel; **19. Sheep**: Ewe, Ram, Lamb, Barn; **20. Pig**: Sow, Boar, Piglet, Sty.

Maths

1. 23.10. LCM (15,25,40) = 600 seconds = 10 minutes, therefore they will snore simultaneously every 10 minutes.

2. The phenomenon reoccurs every 10 minutes and therefore will happen at midnight.

3. 7 times (for example: 23.00, 23.10, 23.20, 23.30, 23.40, 23.50 and 24.00).

4. LCM (10,25,75) = 300 seconds = 5 minutes. They will break wind simultaneously every 5 minutes, so the next time will be at 23.20.

5. LCM (15, 24, 40, 10, 20, 75) = 600 seconds = 10 minutes. From 23.20 onwards, they will snore and break wind in unison every 10 minutes.

6. Let B, R and G represent the number of blue, red and green dresses that Imogen owns, and T the total number of dresses that she owns (T = B + R + G). We know that T – 2 = B, T – 2 = R, T – 2 = G, and therefore 3T – 6 = B + R + G = T. So 2T – 6 = 0, T = 3 and B = R = G = 1. Katy has a single dress in each colour.

p. 31
Geography

1. Thames, 2. Hebrides, 3. Bailey, 4. Portland, 5. Shannon, 6. Sole, 7. Forth, 8. Trafalgar, 9. Biscay, 10. Humber, 11. Tyne, 12. Dover, 13. Fastnet, 14. Plymouth, 15. Fair Isle.

General Culture

1. Gloucester, 2. Gustav Holst, 3. Manchester, 4. Moscow, 5. J.S. Bach, 6. Violin, 7. Wolfgang Amadeus Mozart, 8. Diminuendo, 9. Piano, violin and cello, 10. They are all conductors, 11. New Zealand, 12. Pavarotti, Carreras and Domingo, 13. Camille Saint-Saëns, 14. Three, 15. George Frideric Handel, 16. French, 17. Oboe, 18. Nine, 19. Harpsichord, 20. New World Symphony.

p. 32

From top to bottom, left to right: hazard warning signal light, injection fault indicator light, hand brake indicator light, electronic fault indicator light, oil pressure warning light, airflow to dashboard vents only, windscreen demisting, battery charge warning light, break pad replacement indicator light, rear screen de-icing light, low fuel warning light, horn, sidelight indicator light, ventilator fan, headlight main beam indicator light, rear fog light indicator light, rear screen wash wipe, dipped beam headlight indicator light, hand-brake system warning light, coolant temperature warning light.

Part 4

p. 34
Grammar

1. Kick someone upstairs, 2. Kick against the rules, 3. A kick in the pants, 4. A kick in the teeth, 5. Kick someone when they're down, 6. Kick up a fuss, 7. Kick the habit, 8. Kick the bucket, 9. Kick something around, 10. Kick back, 11. Kick someone out, 12. Kick up your heels.

Literature

1j, 2i, 3h, 4g, 5a, 6f, 7b, 8d, 9c, 10e.

Maths

1. The radius R is equal to half of the diameter D, so 350mm; the perimeter = 3.1416 x 700 mm = 2199.12mm.

2. The surface = 1,539,384mm² = 12,393,84cm² = 1,539,384m².

3. Distance travelled per 1000 revolutions = 2,199,120 mm = 2,199,120 km.

4. 35 km = 35 x 10⁶ mm. The number of revolutions is therefore 35 x 10⁶ / 2199.12 = 0.0159154 x 10⁶ revolutions = 15,915.4 revolutions.

5. When seat no. 87 and no. 103 cross, no. 95 is transitory. When no. 225 and no. 245 cross, no. 235 is transitory. The total number of seats is therefore 2 x (235-95) = 280. Note: to find the number of the transitory seat, you can count on your fingers or draw a little diagram, but the easiest way is to take the average of the 2 seats that are crossing. For example 95 = (87 + 103) / 2, and you can prove that there are the same number of seats between 95 and 87 as between 103 and 95.

p. 35

History

1b3, 2d2, 3a4, 4i7, 5f5, 6c1, 7g10, 8e6, 9h8, 10m12, 11n9, 12l11, 13j14, 14o15, 15k13.

General Culture

1988 (Sabrina Solerno), 1996 (Los del Rio), 1985 (Baltimora), 1997 (Aqua), 1963 (The Beach Boys), 1970 (Mungo Jerry).

p. 36

Literature

1c, 2c, 3c, 4d, 5d, 6a, 7d, 8a, 9c, 10b.

Maths

1. 1 − 1/5 = 5/5 − 1/5 = 4/5.

2. 4/5 x 1/4 = 4/20 = 1/5.

3. When he arrives at his brother's, Phil has 75 x 1/5 = 75/5 = 15 litres left. He uses 16 litres, therefore he's left with −1 litre.

4. Having driven with fuel that he didn't have, he probably left from Lourdes.

5. 8 + 8 + 8 + 88 + 888 = 1,000.

6. 99 days.

p. 37

History

Ancient history: 1b, 2c, 3b, 4a.

Modern history: 1a, 2b, 3b, 4a.

Contemporary history : 1c, 2c, 3a, 4b.

General Culture

Apocalypse Now (1979), *Forrest Gump* (1994), *The Godfather* (1972).

p. 38

Geography

1. Continental/taiga, 2. Mediterranean/scrubland and garrigue,

3. oceanic/moor, 4. tropical/savanna and steppe, 5. polar/tundra, 6. equatorial/rainforest, 7. desert/lack of vegetation, 8. mountainous/ coniferous forest.

Grammar

1d, 2b, 3i, 4c, 5h, 6a, 7f, 8g, 9j, 10e.

Maths

Table: *1 mm* = 0.001m, 1/1,000m, 10⁻³m, 0.000001km, 1/1,000,000km, 10⁻⁶ km. *1 cm* = 0.01m, 1/100m, 10⁻² m, 0.00001km, 1/100,000km, 10⁻⁵ km. *1dm* = 0.1m, 1/10m, 10⁻¹m, 0.0001km, 1/10,000 km, 10⁻⁴km. *1m* = 1, 1, 1, 0.001km, 1/1,000km, 10⁻³ km. 1km = 1,000m, 1,000m, 10³ m, 1, 1, 1.

1. 75 x 10,000cm = 75 x 104cm = 75 x 104 x 10 − 5km = 75 x 10 − 1km = 7.5km.

2. 80 x 1,000,000cm = 80 x 10⁶cm = 80 x 10⁶ x 10 − 5km = 80 x 10km = 800km.

3. 600km, so you'll need a deep glove compartment.

4. Let P be the weight of one melon. We know that 8P/1 = 1/2P. So, 16 P² = 1.4P = 1kg, so P = 250g.

p. 39

General Culture

Top row: Sandro Botticelli, Claude Monet, Amedeo Modigliani.

Second row: Vincent van Gogh, Henri Rousseau, Paul Cézanne.

Third row: Édouard Manet, Piet Mondrian, Edvard Munch.

Bottom row: Paul Gauguin, Egon Schiele, Frida Kahlo.

pp. 40–41

1k, 2j, 3p, 4c, 5a, 6i, 7t, 8e, 9f, 10d, 11o, 12g, 13b, 14h, 15l, 16m, 17n, 18q, 19r, 20s.

Part 5

p. 42

Literature

1e, 2h, 3b, 4j, 5i, 6d, 7a, 8f, 9g, 10c.

Maths

1. Jørgen's speed: 24km/h.

2. 12 minutes, 30 seconds.

3. The problem amounts to calculating how long it would take a person running at 3km/h to cover a distance of 800m, so 16 minutes.

4. As the cyclist and the young woman are moving towards each other, their speeds are added together. The time it takes for them to bump into each other is the same as it would take someone moving at a speed of 30 + 12 = 42 km/h to cover a distance of 1 km, that is 25.71 seconds.

5. As there is twice as much alcohol as water, the total quantity of liquid must be divisible by 3. The total capacity of the six flasks is 137cc, which leaves 2 over when divided by 3. Therefore, the capacity of the empty flask must also leave 2 when it's divided by 3. The only flask that fulfils this criterion is the 23cc one. This is therefore the one that was broken.

The total capacity of the remainder of the flasks is 114cc. One-third of 114cc (in other words 38cc) is filled with water. This means that the 16cc and 22cc flasks are filled with water and the 18cc, 24cc and 34cc ones are filled with alcohol.

p. 43
History
1. 1. keep, 2. loophole, 3. battlements, 4. drawbridge, 5. inner bailey, 6. outer bailey, 7. curtain wall, 8. machicolation, 9. parapet walk, 10. gatehouse.
2. aeroplane, tractor, French flag, wind turbine, inflatable lilo, television aerial, bicycle.

Geography
Top row: Austria, Mali, The Netherlands, Thailand, Ireland. **Middle row:** Côte d'Ivoire, Hungary, Norway, Cameroon, Belgium. **Bottom row:** Costa Rica, Italy, Germany, Poland, Finland.

p. 44
Geography
1. Pacific, 2. Canada, 3. Vatican City, 4. Russia, 5. China, 6. Pacific, 7. Libya, 8. France, 9. China, 10. Angel Falls, 11. Caspian Sea, 12. Nile, 13. Greenland, 14. Sahara, 15. Andes, 16. Suez Canal, 17. Nauru, 18. Rhode Island, 19. Yellow Sea, 20. Lake Baikal.

Maths
1. Thales' theorem applied to the triangle BAA' can be written as $h / a = d^2/(d^1+d^2)$.

Thales' theorem applied to the triangle ABB' can be written as $h / b = d^1/(d^1+d^2)$.

2. From what has already been established, $h/a + h/b = (d^1 + d^2)/ (d^1 + d^2) = 1$. Thus $h(1/a + 1/b) = 1$, so $h = ab/a + b$.

3. The height h is dependent only on the height of the posts.

4. None has three sides of the same colour.

5. Every hour, the difference in the time shown by the two watches increases by 20 minutes. The current time difference shown is 2 hours, or in other words 120 minutes. 120/20 = 6, which means that 6 hours have elapsed since the watches were synchronized. In that time, Eddy's watch has gained 60 minutes (1 hour) and Jake's has lost 60 minutes (1 hour). This means it is now 18.00. (If it's not 18.00 by your watch, get this book checked by a watchmaker.)

p. 45
French
1a, 2b, 3a, 4a, 5b, 6b, 7b, 8b, 9c, 10b, 11c, 12a, 13b, 14c, 15a, 16c, 17a, 18b, 19c, 20a.

General Culture
CIAO: 1988, Italy. *STRIKER:* 1994, United States. *NARANJITO:* 1982, Spain. *TIP ET TAP:* 1974, West Germany. *WILLIE:* 1966, England. *PIQUE:* 1986, Mexico.

p. 46
Grammar
1a, 2a, 3c, 4b, 5c, 6c, 7a, 8b, 9b, 10b, 11a, 12c, 13a, 14b, 15c.

Maths
1. When you throw a dice that isn't loaded, each number has an equal chance of coming up, so the probability of a 6 coming up is 1/6.

The probability that a 6 doesn't come up in 1 throw of the dice is 25/36.

The probability that at least one 6 is thrown is 11/36.

The probability that both die land on a 6 is 1/36.

2. For the 1st place, there are as many choices possible as numbers of horses, that is 8. For 2nd place, there are as many chances as horses left, so 7, and for the 3rd place, there are 6 chances. The possible number of outcomes for 1st, 2nd and 3rd places is therefore 8 x 7 x 6 = 336. The probability of correctly guessing all three places is thus 1/336 = 0.00298.

3. The probability here is 1/56 = 0.0179.

4. In the first glass, with a capacity of C, there is C/2 of wine and C/2 of water. In the second glass, which has a capacity of 2C, there is 1/4 x 2C of wine, or in other words C/2 of wine and 2C – C/2, or 3C/2 of water. In the bowl (remember that it is yellow), there will be a quantity of wine equal to C/2 + C/2, so C, and a quantity of wine C/2 + 3C/2, so 2C. Thus the bowl will contain 1/3 wine and 2/3 water.

p. 47
History
15/07/1099, 16/07/1942, 17/07/1967, 18/07/1925, 19/07/1903, 20/07/1810, 21/07/1969, 22/07/2004, 23/07/1945, 24/07/1534, 25/07/1593, 26/07/1891, 27/07/1214, 28/07/2005, 29/07/1981, 30/07/1980, 31/07/1588,
01/08/1635, 02/08/1990, 03/08/1914, 04/08/1944, 05/08/1897, 06/08/1945, 07/08/1960, 08/08/1908, 09/08/1974, 10/08/1792, 11/08/1999, 12/08/1908, 13/08/1961, 14/08/1947, 15/08/1969.

General Culture
The German.

HOUSE	1	2	3	4	5
COLOUR	yellow	blue	red	green	white
COUNTRY	Norwegian	Dane	Englishman	German	Swede
DRINK	water	tea	milk	coffee	beer
SMOKES	Dunhill	Blend	Pall Mall	Prince	Blue Master
PET	cat	horse	bird	**goldfish**	dog

Calculus on fractions

$$\frac{a}{1} = a; \quad \frac{a}{b} + \frac{c}{b} = \frac{a+c}{b}; \quad \frac{a}{b} \times \frac{c}{d} = \frac{a \times c}{b \times d}; \quad \frac{a}{b} \div \frac{c}{d} = \frac{a}{b} \times \frac{d}{c}; \quad \frac{a \times b}{c \times b} = \frac{a}{c}$$

To divide a fraction by another, multiply the first by the inverse of the other.
The value of a fraction does not change if we multiply or if we divide the numerator and the denominator by the same number. To simplify a fraction, divide its numerator and denominator by the GCD (see below) of these 2 numbers. To add or subtract 2 fractions, reduce them to the same denominator.

$$\frac{a}{b} + \frac{c}{d} = \frac{ab + dc}{bd}$$

Thales' theorem

In the triangle ABC, if I is the mid-point of AB, and J is the mid-point of AC, then IJ is parallel to BC:

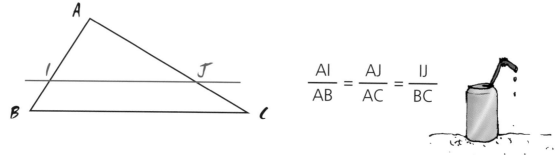

$$\frac{AI}{AB} = \frac{AJ}{AC} = \frac{IJ}{BC}$$

LCM

LCM is the abbreviation of '**Lowest Common Multiple**'. The LCM of 2 whole numbers X and Y – written as LCM (X,Y) – is the smallest whole number that is a multiple of both X and Y. To find this, reduce X and Y into prime factors. LCM (X,Y) is the product of the highest powers of prime factors that feature in at least one of these 2 decompositions.
Ex: $LCM (147,693) = LCM (3 \times 7^2, 3^2 \times 7 \times 11) = 3^2 \times 7^2 \times 11 = 4851$.

GCD

GCD is the abbreviation of '**Greatest Common Divisor**'. The GCD of 2 whole numbers X and Y – written as GCD (X,Y) – is the largest whole number that divides exactly into X and Y. To find this, reduce X and Y into prime factors. GCD (X,Y) is the product of the lowest powers of prime factors common to these 2 decompositions.
Ex: $GCD (147,693) = GCD (3 \times 7^2, 3^2 \times 7 \times 11) = 3 \times 7 = 21$.

Percentages

To calculate the percentage (p) of a number, multiply it by p and divide by 100.
Ex: *To calculate 6% of 35: 35 x 6 / 100 = 2.1.*
If a value S is made bigger by p%, the increase equals S x p / 100 and the new value is S' = S + (S x p / 100) = S (1 + p/100).
So if a salary of £2000 is increased by 6%, the new salary is £2000 x 1.06 = £2120.
Inversely, if a salary of £1800 goes up to £1980, this would correspond to an increase in percentage of 10%.

$$\frac{1980 - 1800}{1800} = 0.10 = 10\%$$

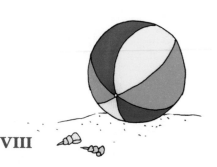

GEOGRAPHY

Can you name each of these cities?

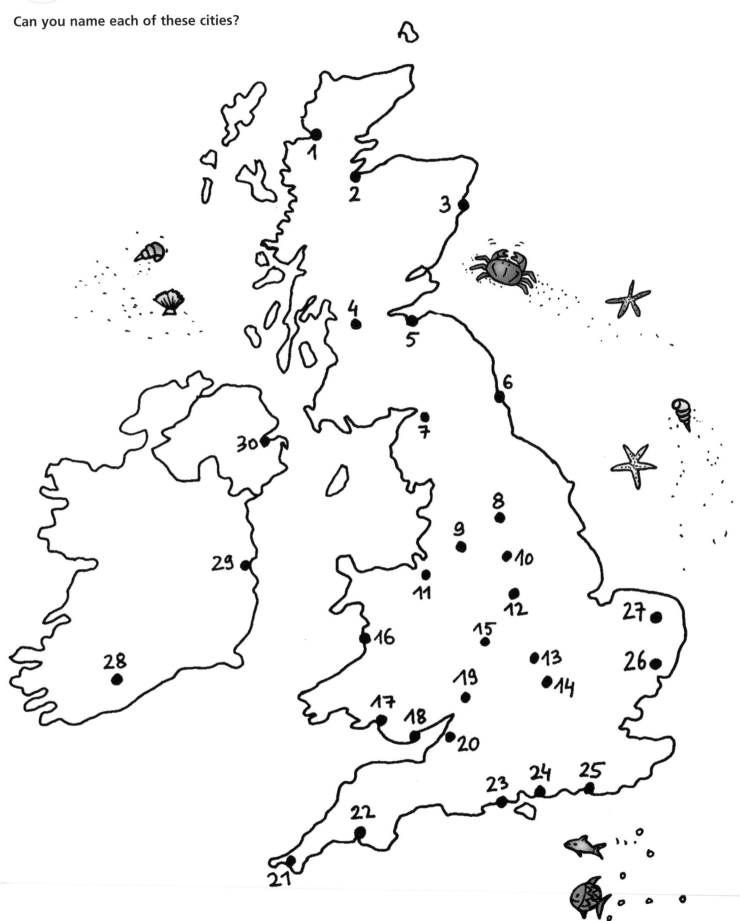

SCIENCE

Give each of the following animals its mother, father, baby and home.
(NB: In some cases there's more than one possible answer.)

	Animal	Female	Male	Baby	Home
1	Bear				
2	Mole	Female	Male		
3	Pigeon				
4	Badger			/	/
5	Lion		Lion		
6	Horse				
7	Otter	Female	Male		
8	Fox			/ /	/
9	Bee				/
10	Eagle	Female	Male		
11	Hare				/
12	Wolf			/	
13	Beaver	Female	Male	/	
14	Mouse			/ /	/
15	Tiger		Tiger	/	
16	Donkey			/	
17	Squirrel			/ /	
18	Dog				
19	Sheep				
20	Pig				

MATHS

Nif-Nif, Naf-Naf and Nouf-Nouf are 3 little pigs who sleep in the same bedroom. They all start snoring at 23.00. Nif-Nif snores every 15 seconds, Naf-Naf every 25 seconds and Nouf-Nouf every 40 seconds.

1 What time will it be when they next snore simultaneously?

2 Will this phenomenon be repeated at midnight?

3 How many times will this phenomenon be repeated in 1 hour?

4 From 23.15, they also begin to break wind. Nif-Nif lets out a fart every 10 seconds, Naf-Naf every 20 seconds and Nouf-Nouf every 75 seconds. When will they fart at the same time again?

5 When, for the first time, will they all snore and break wind at the same time?

 Katy has more than 2 dresses. All but 2 are blue, all but 2 are red, and all but 2 are green. How many dresses does she own in all?

GEOGRAPHY

The shipping forecast is like cricket or bridge – incomprehensible to most of us. Even if you're not one of the initiated, see if you can link the names of the sea areas surrounding the British Isles (listed below) to the following clues:

Bailey, Sole, Portland, Dover, Biscay, Forth, Fair Isle, Thames, Tyne, Trafalgar, Plymouth, Fastnet, Humber, Shannon, Hebrides

1 World's first underwater tunnel built under this river _____
2 Archipelago that includes Islay, Jura, Barra and St. Kilda _____
3 An enclosed courtyard typically overlooked by a motte _____
4 The type of cement used for most mortar and concrete _____
5 Ireland's longest river _____
6 Bottom of a shoe or a flat fish _____
7 River that flows through Stirling and Alloa _____
8 Battle of 21st October 1805 _____
9 Basque province whose capital is Bilbao _____
10 Estuary formed by the Rivers Ouse and Trent _____
11 River that divides Newcastle and Gateshead _____
12 Kent home of the White Cliffs _____
13 608-mile annual yachting race beginning off Cowes _____
14 Football team named Argyle _____
15 Island lying between Shetland and Orkney _____

GENERAL CULTURE

1 The Three Choirs festival involves Hereford, Worcester and which other city?

2 Which British composer is most famous for his orchestral suite *The Planets*?

3 Which city is the home of the Hallé Orchestra?

4 Tchaikovsky's *1812 Overture* commemorates Napoleon's retreat from what city?

5 Which composer wrote six *Brandenburg Concertos*?

6 What instrument does Joshua Bell play professionally?

7 Antonio Salieri was the sworn rival to which 18th century composer?

8 What is 'dim.' the abbreviation for on a musical score?

9 Which instruments usually form a piano trio?

10 What do Sir Colin Davis, Leonard Bernstein and Bernard Haitink have in common?

11 Which country is Kiri Te Kanawa from?

12 What were the surnames of the Three Tenors?

13 In classical music, who composed *The Carnival of the Animals*?

14 How many movements are typically found in a concerto?

15 Who wrote 'The Hallelujah Chorus'?

16 What nationality were the classical composers Berlioz and Ravel?

17 Which instrument plays the 'tuning A' for an orchestra?

18 How many symphonies did Beethoven compose?

19 The spinet and the virginal are both small types of which keyboard instrument?

20 Dvorak's *Symphony No 9* is better known as what symphony?

The dashboard

Note the function of each symbol. To jog your memory, the red indicator lights warn the driver of an urgent problem, the amber ones serve as a reminder that something needs attention, and the green or blue ones show the lights that are on.

The first one to see the sea wins!!

20

The memory of an elephant

This trick, which is 2,500 years old, will help you to memorize any sort of list. Very practical when you're doing the shopping…

1 Link each number with a specific object. For example, the number 1 might make you think of the Eiffel Tower, the number 2 of a pair of glasses, the number 5 of a hand, etc. All of this is very subjective, of course, so it's up to you to choose what you associate each number with. The quirkier or stranger the image, the more likely you are to remember it… Once you've established your list, learn it by heart, and repeat it as often as possible until each number immediately evokes your associated image.

2 Train yourself to memorize imaginary lists, then, when you feel that you're ready, ask anyone to write a list of any 20 objects, to read it to you once, number by number, and then to ask you to recite these objects in the order of his or her choice. Astounded by your elephantine memory, your friends will no doubt want to try this themselves, but there's not much chance they'll succeed… Make the most of your moment of glory when they beg you to explain the trick…

My list of references

1 _____
2 _____
3 _____
4 _____
5 _____
6 _____
7 _____
8 _____
9 _____
10 _____
11 _____
12 _____
13 _____
14 _____
15 _____
16 _____
17 _____
18 _____
19 _____
20 _____

change your look

Holidays are the ideal time to give yourself a new look. Try out some of these ideas on our models!

Chinstrap
A short beard that grows all along the jawline, even on the chin.

Stubble
Hair barely covers the chin, the cheeks and the jaw – the three-day beard.

Van Dyck
A goatee with an (uncon-nected) moustache.

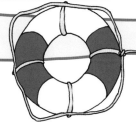

Hollywoodian
A moustache grows right round the mouth to join a small, neat beard.

Handlebar moustache
A long moustache that covers the lip and points outwards.

Sideburns
Facial hair comes down the cheeks, sometimes even as far as the jawline.

Full beard
Facial hair completely covers the chin, the cheeks and the jaw.

Goatee
A tuft of hairs sprouts from the chin (no moustache).

# &GRAMMAR

Rewrite the following sentences using expressions containing the word 'kick':

1 Promote someone to a higher but effectively powerless position

2 Express resentment against authority

3 Something that prompts or forces renewed effort

4 Receive a (humiliating) blow or setback

5 Cause more suffering to someone who's already struggling

6 Object forcefully or loudly about something

7 Free oneself of an addiction

8 Die

9 Casually or informally discuss (an idea)

10 Enjoy yourself without inhibitions

11 Show someone the door

12 Relax

LITERATURE

Match the following Shakespeare quotations and plays:

Twelfth Night 1 • • A It is a wise father that knows his own child

Hamlet, Prince of Denmark 2 • • B Ill met by moonlight, proud Titania

Julius Caesar 3 • • C What's in a name? That which we call a rose by any other name would smell as sweet

King John 4 • • D Now is the winter of our discontent

The Merchant of Venice 5 • • E But I will wear my heart upon my sleeve

Macbeth 6 • • F Double, double toil and trouble; Fire burn, and cauldron bubble

A Midsummer Night's Dream 7 • • G To gild refined gold, to paint the lily

King Richard III 8 • • H Et tu, Brute?

Romeo and Juliet 9 • • I Brevity is the soul of wit

Othello, the Moor of Venice 10 • • J If music be the food of love, play on

# MATHS

Charlie has a bicycle with wheels of 700mm diameter.

1 Calculate the radius and the circumference of one of Charlie's bicycle wheels.

2 One of Charlie's bicycle wheels is convex (disk wheel). What is its surface in mm², in cm² et in m²?

3 How far will Charlie have cycled after 1000 revolutions of his bicycle wheels?

4 How many revolutions will the wheels have made when Charlie has cycled for 35km?

The seats of the chairlift at Val-Boutrangue are spaced regularly and numbered in order starting at no. 1. At the moment when seat no. 87 crosses with no. 103, seat no. 225 crosses with no. 245. How many seats are there on the chairlift? (Assume that there is a transitory seat between the one completing the climb and the one at the start of the descent, as well as one between the seat arriving at the bottom and one beginning its ascent.)

HISTORY

Link each war film with its corresponding conflict and dates:

Film		Conflict		Dates	
Gone with the Wind	1 •	• A Hundred Years' War	A •	• 1 1957–75	
Hotel Rwanda	2 •	• B American Civil War	B •	• 2 1994	
Joan of Arc	3 •	• C Vietnam War	C •	• 3 1861–5	
The Killing Fields	4 •	• D Rwandan Genocide	D •	• 4 1337–1453	
Black Hawk Down	5 •	• E Seven Years' War	E •	• 5 1993	
Apocalypse Now	6 •	• F Somali Civil War	F •	• 6 1754–61	
Gallipoli	7 •	• G First World War	G •	• 7 1967–75	
Barry Lindon	8 •	• H Korean War	H •	• 8 1950–3	
M*A*S*H	9 •	• I Cambodian Civil War	I •	• 9 1939–45	
Land and Freedom	10 •	• J Battle of Thermopylae	J •	• 10 1914–18	
Saving Private Ryan	11 •	• K Gulf War	K •	• 11 1992–5	
No Man's Land	12 •	• L Bosnian War	L •	• 12 1936–9	
300	13 •	• M Spanish Civil War	M •	• 13 1991	
The Hunt for Red October	14 •	• N Second World War	N •	• 14 480BC	
Three Kings	15 •	• O Cold War	O •	• 15 1947–89	

GENERAL CULTURE

Find the year and name the group of these summertime hits:

Boys

Rain Man, starring Tom Cruise and Dustin Hoffman, is released. Wimbledon wins the FA Cup. The USSR begins withdrawal from Afghanistan. A terrorist bomb brings down a Pan-Am 747 over Lockerbie. General Zia of Pakistan is killed in a plane crash.

Year _____

Group _____

Macarena

The English Patient, written and directed by Anthony Minghella, is released. Sri Lanka wins the cricket World Cup. Dolly the Sheep is born. Yasser Arafat is elected first President of Palestine. Death of American rapper Tupac Shakur.

Year _____

Group _____

Tarzan Boy

Out of Africa, starring Robert Redford and Meryl Streep, is released. Mohammed Al-Fayed buys Harrods. Military coup removes Milton Obote from power in Uganda. *Achille Lauro* is hijacked by terrorists. Mikhail Gorbachev becomes Soviet leader.

Year _____

Group _____

Barbie Girl

Titanic is released. Gianni Versace is murdered. Diana, Princess of Wales is killed in a car crash. New Zealand's first ever female prime minister is sworn in. Tony Blair wins a landslide election victory.

Year _____

Group _____

Surfin' USA

Dr. No, the first James Bond film, is released. Spy Kim Philby flees to Moscow. The Great Train Robbery takes place. Doctor Beeching's report means harsh cuts in Britain's railways. President Kennedy is assassinated.

Year _____

Group _____

In The Summertime

Patton, starring George C. Scott, is released. Jimi Hendrix dies. Brazil wins the football World Cup. President Nasser of Egypt dies. Pope Paul VI survives an assassination attempt.

Year _____

Group _____

LITERATURE

Name the odd one out from these lists:

1 All are plays by Shakespeare except....
a. Macbeth
b. King Lear
c. Socrates
d. Titus Andronicus

2 All are Agatha Christie characters except...
a. Miss Marple
b. Tommy and Tuppence
c. Nancy Drew
d. Hercule Poirot

3 All are pigs in *Animal Farm* except...
a. Old Major
b. Squealer
c. Mr. Whymper
d. Minimus

4 All are Christmas books by Charles Dickens except...
a. *The Chimes*
b. *The Battle of Life*
c. *The Cricket on the Hearth*
d. *A Christmas Tale*

5 All are Beatrix Potter rabbits except...
a. Peter
b. Flopsy
c. Mopsy
d. Tom

6 All are James Bond stories by Ian Fleming except...
a. *Goldeneye*
b. *Quantum of Solace*
c. *Risico*
d. *The Hildebrand Rarity*

7 All appear in *Charlie and the Chocolate Factory* except...
a. Mike Teavee
b. Veruca Salt
c. Violet Beauregarde
d. Matilda Wormwood

8 All are fictional horses except...
a. Aslan
b. Rocinante
c. The Pie
d. Fru-Fru

9 All have won the Nobel Prize for Literature except...
a. Doris Lessing
b. Günter Grass
c. Salman Rushdie
d. Harold Pinter

10 All tell tales in Chaucer's *Canterbury Tales* except...
a. Physician
b. Alchemist
c. Shipman
d. Reeve

MATHS

The fuel tank of Phil's car contains 75 litres. On the way to his holiday destination, he uses one-fifth of this to go and see his sister Ruby. (To respect their privacy, we have changed the names of the protagonists in this exercise.)

1 What fraction of a full tank is he left with?
2 He uses three-quarters of what is left to go and visit his brother Jack. What fraction of a full tank is he left with now?
3 He uses up a further 16 litres of fuel to get to his final destination, Torquay. How many litres of fuel are now left in the tank?
4 Work out his town of departure from this information.

 How can you obtain 1000 by adding only numbers that contain 8?

 A water lily in a pond doubles in size every day. It would take 100 days for it to spread across the whole of the pond. How many days would it take to cover half the water's surface?

HISTORY

What sort of historian are you? Here's a quiz that will enable you to answer this essential question...

Ancient history

1 What was the capital of Lower Egypt?
a. Nashville
b. Memphis
c. Thebes

2 Which of these animals was not an Egyptian divinity?
a. Frog
b. Goose
c. Elephant

3 Of which of these philosophers was Socrates a contemporary?
a. Aristotle
b. Confucius
c. Spinoza

4 How does Antigone die in the play of the same name by Sophocles?
a. She is buried alive
b. She is burnt alive
c. She is impaled

Modern history

1 Christopher Columbus had three caravels: the Pinta, the Santa Maria and...
a. The Niña
b. The Isabella
c. The Comparsita

2 Which city symbolizes the Renaissance?
a. Paris
b. Florence
c. Athens

3 Which king of France authorized Protestantism in 1498?
a. Henri III
b. Henri IV
c. Louis XIII

4 How did King Charles I die in 1649?
a. He was beheaded
b. He was guillotined
c. He died in his sleep

Contemporary history

1 Where was the German Empire proclaimed in 1871?
a. Weimar
b. Berlin
c. Versailles

2 In which battle in 1916 were more than 1 million soldiers killed?
a. The Battle of Verdun
b. The Battle of Jutland
c. The Battle of the Somme

3 Who was the British Prime Minister at the outbreak of World War II?
a. Neville Chamberlain
b. Winston Churchill
c. Clement Attlee

4 Which of these French presidents held office for the longest time?
a. Charles de Gaulle
b. François Mitterrand
c. Jacques Chirac

GENERAL CULTURE

Find the titles of these films from the quotes and details of their posters
(bonus points to those who can name their release dates, within two years):

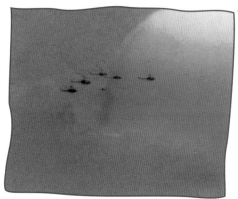

I love the smell of napalm in the morning

Life is like a box of chocolates... you never know what you're gonna get.

I'm going to make him an offer he can't refuse...

GEOGRAPHY

What climate do the following animals live in? And what type of habitat corresponds with this climate?

Tropical – oceanic – continental – equatorial – polar – mediterranean – desert – mountainous

Wolf – brown bear: _____ *1*
Scorpionfish – cicada: _____ *2*
Seagull – hedgehog: _____ *3*
Giraffe – zebra: _____ *4*
Polar bear – lemming: _____ *5*
Tapir – toucan: _____ *6*
Fennec fox – dromedary: _____ *7*
Marmot – ibex: _____ *8*

- rainforest
- savanna and steppe
- tundra
- taiga
- coniferous forest
- scrubland and garrigue
- moor
- lack of vegetation

&GRAMMAR

Assign the right meaning to each Latin phrase:

Acta est fabula *1* •
Ad vitam aeternam *2* •
Cogito ergo sum *3* •
Si vis pacem, para bellum *4* •
Sol lucet omnibus *5* •
Dura lex, sed lex *6* •
Mens sana in corpore sano *7* •
Errare humanum est *8* •
Fluctuat nec mergitur *9* •
In vino veritas *10* •

- *A* The law is harsh, but it is the law
- *B* For all time
- *C* If you want peace, prepare for the war
- *D* The play is over
- *E* The truth is in wine
- *F* A sound mind in a sound body
- *G* To err is human
- *H* The sun shines upon us all
- *I* I think, therefore I am
- *J* It is tossed by the waves but it does not sink

MATHS

Complete this table which shows conversions of millimetres (mm), centimetres (cm), decimetres (dm), metres (m) and kilometres (km) into metres and kilometres. What? Yes, just complete the table, please.

	metres		*kilometres*	
1mm	0,001			
1cm		10^{-2}		
1dm		1/10		
1m				
1km				

1 On a 1/10,000 scale map, the distance between two towns is 75cm. What is the actual distance between these two towns?

2 On a 1/1,000,000 scale map, the distance between two towns is 80cm. What is the actual distance between these two towns?

3 If two towns are 150km apart, how far apart will they be on a 4x scale map?

Olivia's set of scales are wrong: one of the arms is longer than the other. A 1kg weight in the lefthand pan weighs exactly the same as 8 melons in the righthand one. But 1kg in the righthand pan weighs the same as only 2 melons in the lefthand pan. Assuming that all the melons weigh the same, what is the weight of each?

GENERAL CULTURE

Are you an art aficionado? Can you match the artists with details of their famous paintings?

Sandro Botticelli, Paul Cézanne, Paul Gauguin, Vincent van Gogh, Frida Kahlo, Edouard Manet, Amedeo Modigliani, Piet Mondrian, Claude Monet, Edvard Munch, Henri Rousseau, Egon Schiele.

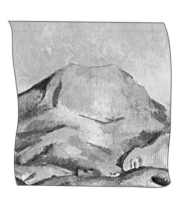

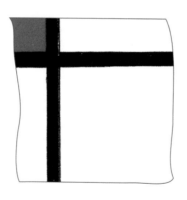

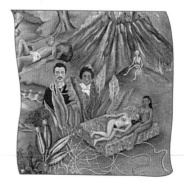

Often, a hand sign speaks louder than words, and the Italians know all about gesticulation. See if you can match each gesture below with its correct meaning, then have fun using them as often as possible! Il conto per favore !

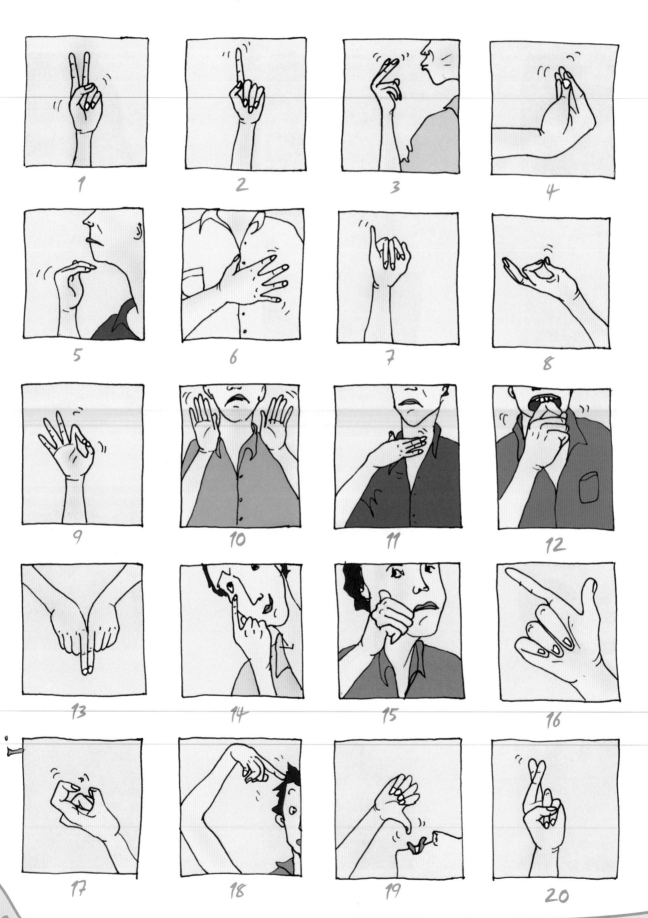

1

2

3

4

5

6

7

8

9

10

11

12

13

14

15

16

17

18

19

20

a. Non me ne importa
I don't care
The fingers flick outwards from under the chin.

b. Se l'intendono
A secret liaison
The two index fingers are pressed together side by side to indicate that two people are getting along extremely well together…

c. Che vuoi ?
What do you think?!
With tips of the fingers touching, the hand is waved up and down, fast or slowly, depending on the degree of impatience being expressed.

d. Io non so niente
It's no concern of mine
This gesture signifies 'it's none of my business', 'I wash my hands of it', or 'I can't do anything about it'.

e. Excellente !
Excellent!
This gesture expresses both appreciation and satisfaction and is one that is typically used by a satisfied gourmet.

f. Tutto bene
Perfect
This gesture is more American than Italian. The thumb and index finger form a circle and the other fingers are stretched out.

g. Rabbia
Rage
To express frustration, make as if to bite the knuckle of your index finger with your front teeth.

h. Intesa
My eye!
The straight index finger positioned just under the eye can mean 'we understand each other', 'I'm watching you', or 'I don't believe that for one minute'.

i. Parola d'onore
On my honour
The hand is placed flat against the chest.

j. Un momento
One moment
The index finger is raised straight in the air to indicate that you require the attention of the person to whom you are speaking.

k. Bisogno Fisico Urgente
I really need to go
To ask for permission to leave the classroom, the hand is raised straight up in the air, the index and middle fingers forming a V.

l. È un dritto
Crafty!
Stroke your cheek with your thumb, from ear to mouth, to show that you think what you're hearing is clever.

m. Niente !
Negation and helplessness
The hand turns from left to right from the wrist to signify 'I don't know', 'I haven't got it', or 'I can't do it'. This is a typical Neapolitan gesture.

n. Vieni qui !
Come here!
The index finger is pointed at the person to whom you are speaking and then bent towards you to call him or her to you.

o. Minaccia
Menace
With your hand flat, palm facing down, execute a rapid movement as if cutting your own throat. This gesture features in all Martin Scorcese's films.

p. Fumare
Do you have a cigarette ?
The index and middle fingers hold an imaginary cigarette. If the person to whom you're making the request doesn't get the message, move the 'cigarette' towards your lips.

q. Idea !
I've got an idea!
The index finger points to the part of the body where ideas are supposedly born: the brain.

r. Bere
Drink
The hand makes a fist with the thumb stretched out to represent the neck of a bottle. This gesture is especially effective if you lean your head back and make as if to pour the drink down your throat.

s. Bugia
Fingers crossed!
This international gesture signifies that the person doesn't believe what he or she is saying (or perhaps doesn't want to believe it).

t. Magro così
This skinny
The little finger is held up to indicate thinness.

41

&GRAMMAR

The zeugma is a figure of speech in which a word is applied to two or more others with different senses.
For example: *He carried his rucksack and the responsibility for the walk.* **Have fun finishing these sentences!**

The teacher ate his words and _____

Pete felt confusion and _____

The old man dragged his old bones and _____

He threw in the towel and _____

We took the train and _____

She pulled up her minidress and _____

He's twiddling his thumbs and _____

The young boy received a punishment and _____

She climbed the stairs and _____

Holly ran a bath and _____

I like playing cards and _____

Stuart decided to take my counsel and _____

LITERATURE

What type of animal are the following Beatrix Potter characters?

Mr Tod **1** •	• **A** Hedgehog
Samuel Whiskers **2** •	• **B** Frog
Jeremy Fisher **3** •	• **C** Owl
Timmy Tiptoes **4** •	• **D** Dog
Miss Moppet **5** •	• **E** Fox
Pickles **6** •	• **F** Mouse
Mrs Tiggy-Winkle **7** •	• **G** Rabbit
Hunca Munca **8** •	• **H** Rat
Flopsy **9** •	• **I** Cat
Old Brown **10** •	• **J** Squirrel

MATHS

When he's on form and on the track, Swedish champion Jørgen Chkteflü can run the 100 metres in 11 seconds.

1 Convert his speed to km/h.

2 Express in minutes and seconds the time he would take to run 5000 metres at an average speed of 24km/h.

3 Jørgen is running in a park in Stockholm at a speed of 15km/h. Suddenly he notices, 800m ahead of him, Kirstèn Hoegaarden, a beautiful blonde who is running in the same direction as him but at 12km/h. How long will it take him to reach her?

4 A cyclist who is 1km away from Kirstèn is heading towards her at a speed of 30km/h. How long will it be before he hits her?

For his chemistry class, Henry arranges six small flasks with capacities of 16cc, 18cc, 22cc, 23cc, 24cc and 34cc respectively. He breaks one flask while sneezing and fills the others with either water or alcohol. Eric is taking part in the lesson, but he is blind. 'Which flask did the teacher break? Which flasks has he used for water and which are filled with alcohol?', he asks Jerry, who's sitting next to him. Unfortunately for Eric, Jerry doesn't like helping others. He simply replies, 'There's twice as much alcohol as water in the flasks.' 'Oh, I get it', exclaims Eric, cheerfully. Do you?

42

HISTORY

Correctly place the following terms:

drawbridge, keep, curtain wall, battlements, parapet walk, inner bailey, gatehouse, loophole, machicolation, outer bailey.

1 _____
2 _____
3 _____
4 _____
5 _____
6 _____
7 _____
8 _____
9 _____
10 _____

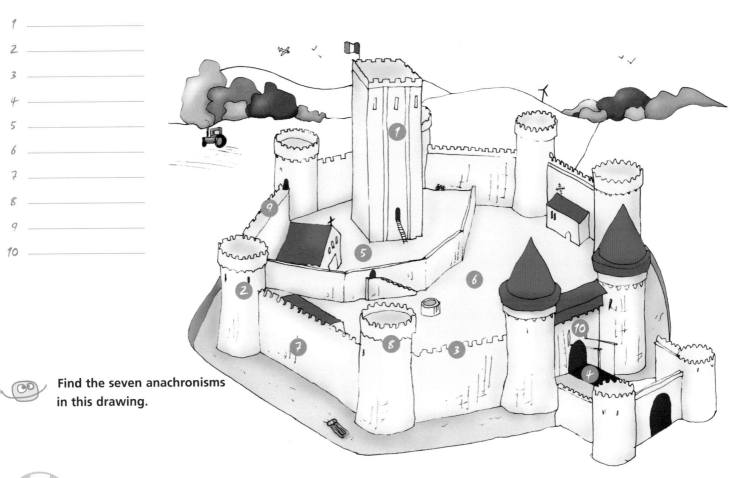

Find the seven anachronisms in this drawing.

GEOGRAPHY

Which country does each of these flags represent:
Germany / Austria / Belgium / Cameroon / Costa Rica / Côte d'Ivoire / Finland / Hungary / Ireland / Italy / Mali / Norway / The Netherlands / Poland / Thailand

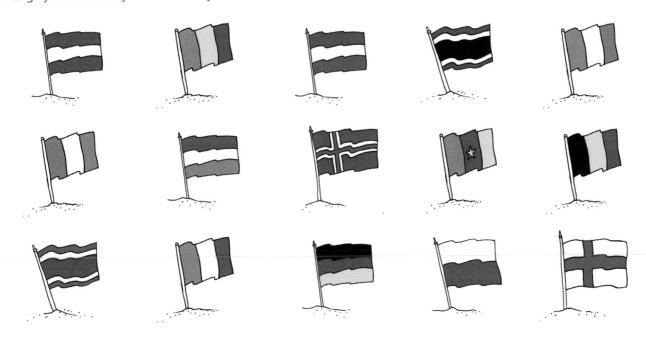

GEOGRAPHY

Can you pick the geographical 'record-breakers' from these choices?

1 Biggest ocean
Atlantic • Indian • Pacific • Arctic

2 Country with the longest coastline
Canada • Brazil • Indonesia • Greenland

3 Smallest independent state
Liechtenstein • Nauru • Monaco • Vatican City

4 Largest country
Russia • Canada • Brazil • China

5 Country with the biggest population
China • India • Bangladesh • Brazil

6 Deepest ocean or sea
Atlantic • Pacific • Bering Sea • Mediterranean Sea

7 Country with the longest official name
Iraq • Sri Lanka • Libya • United Kingdom

8 Country visited by most tourists
United States • Spain • Italy • France

9 Biggest coal producer
Russia • China • Kazakhstan • Bangladesh

10 Highest waterfall
Angel Falls • Tugela • Ostre Mardola Falls • Niagara

11 Largest lake
Sargasso Sea • Lake Superior • Caspian Sea • Aral Sea

12 Longest river
Amazon • Mississippi • Nile • Danube

13 Largest island
Madagascar • Greenland • Sumatra • Borneo

14 Largest desert
Kalahari • Sahara • Simpson • Gobi

15 Longest mountain range
Andes • Pyrenees • Himalayas • Rockies

16 Longest canal
Welland Canal • Panama Canal • Kielder Canal • Suez Canal

17 Smallest island country
Nauru • Tuvalu • Palau • St. Vincent and the Grenadines

18 Smallest U.S. state
Delaware • Connecticut • Rhode Island • Hawaii

19 Shallowest sea
Baltic Sea • North Sea • Red Sea • Yellow Sea

20 Deepest lake
Lake Baikal • Lake Tanganyika • Caspian Sea • Lake Malawi

MATHS

To measure his height, the singer Prince has fixed lasers at the top of two posts (shown here in blue), of which he knows the respective heights a and b. After some tedious adjustments, 'The Artist' manages to get the laser beams to intersect at point I, which coincides with the top of his head if he stands upright at H. The aim of this exercise is to determine the height of 'Love Symbol' as a function of a and b. You can either try to solve the problem on your own, or by answering each of the following questions:

1 Apply Thales' theorum to the triangle BAA', then to the triangle ABB'.

2 What does the sum $\frac{h}{a} + \frac{h}{b}$ equal?

3 Deduce from this that the height h is not dependent on the distance between the two posts.

4 What can be noted about the triangles A'AI, BIB' and AIB?

Eddy's watch gives the time as 19.00, but it is gaining 10 minutes an hour. Jake's shows 17.00 but is losing 10 minutes an hour. Eddy and Jake sychronized their watches to the correct time earlier in the day. What is the time now?

FRENCH

Translate the following words. Attention aux faux-amis !!!

1 Fabric
a. Tissu
b. Usine
c. Artisanat

2 Actually
a. Actuellement
b. En fait
c. Réellement

3 To advertise
a. Faire de la pub
b. Avertir
c. Menacer

4 Appointment
a. Rendez-vous
b. Ajustement
c. Mise au point

5 Conductor
a. Chauffeur
b. Chef d'orchestre
c. Chef de file

6 Clerk
a. Curé
b. Employé
c. Comptable

7 Accommodation
a. Toilettes
b. Logement
c. Arrangement

8 Directory
a. Directoire
b. Annuaire
c. Dictature

9 Eventually
a. Provisoirement
b. Éventuellement
c. Finalement

10 To attire
a. Attirer
b. Vêtir
c. Séduire

11 Agenda
a. Répertoire
b. Agenda
c. Ordre du jour

12 Issue
a. Point
b. Sortie
c. Insertion

13 Library
a. Librairie
b. Bibliothèque
c. Maison d'édition

14 To deride
a. Dérider
b. Dériver
c. Railler

15 Effective
a. Efficace
b. Utile
c. Indispensable

16 To entertain
a. Entraîner
b. Entretenir
c. Divertir

17 Furniture
a. Meubles
b. Fournitures
c. Tapis de souris

18 Journey
a. Journée
b. Voyage
c. Aurore

19 To resign
a. Se résigner
b. Signer à nouveau
c. Démissioner

20 Mess
a. Désordre
b. Restaurant
c. Messe

GENERAL CULTURE

For each mascot, find the year and the host country of the Football World Cup:

Roger Milla (at 38 years old) and Cameroon reach the quarterfinals. The discovery of the championship is the Italian Toto Schillaci, top striker of the competition. Germany wins the Cup after an uninspiring final.

Year _____ / Country _____

Ciao

Striker

For the first time, victory is won in a penalty shootout. Maradona is banned from the championship after he fails a drugs test. Roger Milla becomes the oldest striker in the history of the World Cup (at 42 years old).

Year _____ / Country _____

Diego Maradona plays in his first World Cup. Hungary humiliates Salvador 10–1. Paolo Rossi is the best striker of the championship, scoring 6 goals.

Year _____ / Country _____

Naranjito

Tip and Tap

Johan Cruyff's Netherlands team loses 2–1 in the finals to the hosts. With 7 goals, Grzegorz Lato (Poland) finishes as the top striker. Yugoslavia crush Zaire 9–0.

Year _____ / Country _____

To general shock, Pelé's Brazil is eliminated in the first round. North Korea surprise everyone by qualifying for the quarterfinals. Portuguese Eusebio notches up 9 goals and is the brightest star of this World Cup.

Year _____ / Country _____

Willie

Pique

France beat Brazil in an unforgettable match at the Guadalajara stadium. Maradona scores a goal with his hand against England – the famous 'hand of God'. Argentina wins its 2nd World Cup.

Year _____ / Country _____

45

&GRAMMAR

Match the correct definition to the word:

1 Cyclostome
a. A fishlike jawless vertebrate
b. A curved wall at the rear of a stage
c. An instrument for measuring circular arcs

2 Ethmoid
a. A square bone at the root of the nose
b. A corrosive used in sketching
c. An organic liquid

3 Perorate
a. To spend the night
b. To penetrate throughout
c. To speak at length

4 Mennonite
a. A crescent-shaped figure
b. A member of a Protestant sect
c. A seven-armed candelabrum used in Jewish worship

5 Impolder
a. Burst inwards
b. Put into danger
c. Reclaim from the sea

6 Gobemouche
a. An East Asian warehouse
b. A mine or source of wealth
c. A gullible listener

7 Heliocentric
a. Regarding the sun as centre
b. An apparatus used for photographing the sun
c. A sun worshipper

8 Junker
a. An untidy person
b. A young German nobleman
c. A dish of sweetened and flavoured curds

9 Laterite
a. A triangular sail
b. Clay used for making roads in the Tropics
c. A communal lavatory

10 Simurg
a. An image of something
b. A monstrous bird of Persian myth
c. A hot, dry dust-laden wind

11 Tallow
a. Melted down animal fat used in making candles
b. A scarf worn by Jews at prayer
c. A tall Indian palm

12 Usury
a. To seize or assume wrongfully
b. An amphibian with a tail
c. The practice of lending money at interest

13 Buccinator
a. A flat thin cheek muscle
b. An unscrupulous adventurer
c. A horse-drawn vehicle with a plank body fixed to the axles

14 Actinia
a. Serving temporarily or on the behalf of another
b. A sea anemone
c. A radioactive metallic element

15 Chondrite
a. A basic organic compound occurring widely in living matter
b. A type of short-sleeved bodice worn by Indian women
c. A stony meteorite

MATHS

Matthew, Mark, Luke and John are undecided whether to believe in God.
'Let's throw a dice', suggests Matthew. 'If it's a 6, I will believe in God.'
'Let's throw 2', says Luke, raising the bid. 'If at least one is a 6, I will believe in God.'
'I'll believe if neither is a 6', says John.
'And me', states Mark, 'I will believe in God if both land on 6.'
And they throw the dice.

1 What is the probability associated with each of these strategies?

2 Luke has changed his mind. He now says he will believe if he manages to guess, in the correct order, which horses will finish first, second and third in the race that's about to be broadcast on the radio. There are eight horses racing.
What's the probability that he will believe in God at the end of the race?

3 Luke now says he will believe if he manages to guess correctly the first three horses, in any order. What are the chances that he'll believe in God at the finish?

_____

_____

And what happens to the bottle?

A wine glass is half full of wine. A second glass, with double the capacity of the first one, is a quarter full of wine. Both glasses are then filled to the brim with water, then emptied into a yellow plastic bowl. What is the proportion of wine in this new mixture?

46

HISTORY

It happened over the summer... but in which of the following years?

Dates to fill in:

1099 – 1214 – 1534 – 1588 – 1593 – 1635 – 1792 – 1810 – 1891 – 1897 – 1903 – 1908 (2) – 1914 – 1925 – 1942 – 1944 –
1945 (2) – 1947 – 1960 – 1961 – 1967 – 1969 (2) – 1974 – 1980 – 1981 – 1990 – 1999 – 2004 – 2005

July

15 _____ : the crusaders take Jerusalem
16 _____ : roundup of Jews in the Paris Vélodrome d'Hiver
17 _____ : death of John Coltrane
18 _____ : publication of Adolf Hitler's *Mein Kampf*
19 _____ : arrival of the first Tour de France
20 _____ : declaration of independance of Colombia
21 _____ : Neil Armstrong and Buzz Aldrin land on the Moon
22 _____ : death of Sacha Distel
23 _____ : opening of the trial of Marshal Pétain
24 _____ : conquest of Canada by Jacques Cartier
25 _____ : Henri IV of France converts to Roman Catholicism
26 _____ : France annexes Tahiti
27 _____ : the Battle of Bouvines
28 _____ : end of the armed campaign of the PIRA
29 _____ : marriage of Prince Charles and Lady Diana
30 _____ : Jerusalem becomes the capital of Israel
31 _____ : the Spanish Armada is spotted off the English coast

August

1 _____ : Guadeloupe becomes a French colony
2 _____ : beginning of the Gulf War
3 _____ : Germany declares war on France
4 _____ : Jewish diarist Anne Frank is arrested
5 _____ : first promotional film by Edison
6 _____ : American nuclear bomb lands on Hiroshima
7 _____ : independance of Côte d'Ivoire
8 _____ : the Wright Brothers' first public flight
9 _____ : resignation of Richard Nixon
10 _____ : Louis XVI is arrested
11 _____ : the most recent total eclipse of the sun
12 _____ : launch of the Model T Ford
13 _____ : construction of the Berlin Wall
14 _____ : foundation of Pakistan
15 _____ : first Woodstock festival

GENERAL CULTURE

The ultimate test: Einstein's enigma!
Apparently, 98 % of people who have tried to solve this puzzle finish up beating their heads against a wall.
Are you one of the 2% on our planet with a logical brain? A word of advice before you begin: arm yourself
with lots of patience and a pile of scrap paper...

You are in front of five houses of different colours. The occupiers of these houses are all of different nationalities. Each person favours a particular drink, smokes a different type of cigarette and owns a different sort of pet from the others. The question is simple:

Who owns a goldfish?

The Englishman lives in a red house.
The Swede has a dog.
The Dane drinks tea.
The green house is on the left of the white one.
The owner of the green house drinks coffee.
The person who smokes Pall Malls has a bird.
The owner of the yellow house smokes Dunhills.
The person who lives in the middle house drinks milk.
The Norwegian lives in the first house.

The person who smokes Blends lives next door to the person who owns a cat.
The person who owns a horse lives next door to the person who smokes Dunhills.
The person who smokes Blue Masters also drinks beer.
The German smokes Princes.
The Norwegian lives next door to the blue house.
The person who smokes Blends lives next to the person who drinks water.

3 5 7 9 10 8 6 4

Published in 2008 by Ebury Press, an imprint of Ebury Publishing

A Random House Group Company

First published in France in 2007 by Chiflet & Cie

Copyright © Chiflet & Cie 2007
Translation copyright © Ebury Press 2008

The Random House Group Limited Reg. No. 954009

Addresses for companies within the Random House Group can be found at
www.randomhouse.co.uk

A CIP catalogue record for this book is available from the British Library

The Random House Group Limited supports The Forest Stewardship Council (FSC®),
the leading international forest certification organisation. Our books carrying the
FSC label are printed on FSC® certified paper. FSC is the only forest certification
scheme endorsed by the leading environmental organisations, including Greenpeace.
Our paper procurement policy can be found at www.randomhouse.co.uk/environment

To buy books by your favourite authors and register for offers visit www.randomhouse.co.uk

Printed and bound in Italy by Printer Trento SRL

ISBN 9780091927585

CREDITS

Illustrations by Raphaëlle d'Hautefeuille

Original design by Stéphanie Aguado

English edition project managed and translated by Anne McDowall

Additional question for English edition by Freequizzes